THE BELFAST GUIDELINES ON AMNESTY AND ACCOUNTABILITY
WITH EXPLANATORY GUIDANCE

The Nuffield Foundation is an endowed charitable trust that aims to improve social well-being in the widest sense. It funds research and innovation in education and social policy and also works to build capacity in education, science and social science research. The Nuffield Foundation has funded this project, but the views expressed are those of the authors and not necessarily those of the Foundation.
More information is available at www.nuffieldfoundation.org

Published and disseminated by the Transitional Justice Institute at the University of Ulster

Please feel free to copy any information from this booklet; reference to the source would be appreciated.

ISBN: 978-1-85923-261-3

© Transitional Justice Institute, University of Ulster 2013

Printed in Belfast, Northern Ireland

Guidelines are also translated into Arabic, French, Mandarin, Russian and Spanish.

All language versions and Explanatory Guidance also available electronically at: www.ulster.ac.uk/transitionaljustice

For further information, please contact
Dr Louise Mallinder
Transitional Justice Institute
University of Ulster
Shore Road
Newtownabbey
BT37 0QB
Email: l.mallinder@ulster.ac.uk

Designed by Pierce Communications

CONTENTS

The Belfast Guidelines on Amnesty and Accountability 1

INTRODUCTION 1

    Aims of the Guidelines 1

    Expert Group Composition 1

    The Evidence Base 4

PART A. GENERAL PRINCIPLES 6

    Guideline 1. Balancing States' Multiple Obligations and Objectives in Protecting Human Rights 6

    Guideline 2. Accountability 7

    Guideline 3. The Role of Prosecutions 8

    Guideline 4. The Role of Amnesties 9

    Guideline 5. Linking Amnesty with Accountability 10

PART B. SCOPE OF AMNESTIES 10

    Guideline 6. Amnesties and International Obligations to Prosecute 10

    Guideline 7. Eligible Offences 12

    Guideline 8. Eligible Beneficiaries 13

    Guideline 9. Temporal Scope 16

    Guideline 10. Geographic Scope 16

PART C. AMNESTY CONDITIONS 17

Guideline 11. Prior Conditions on Amnesty Beneficiaries 17

Guideline 12. Conditions of Future Conduct on
Amnesty Beneficiaries 18

PART D. AMNESTY ADOPTION, IMPLEMENTATION
AND REVIEW 19

Guideline 13. Adherence to Domestic Law 19

Guideline 14. Method of Enactment and
Public Consultation 19

Guideline 15. Legal Effects 21

Guideline 16. Administering the Amnesty 22

Guideline 17. Annulling Amnesties 23

Guideline 18. International Courts and
National Amnesties 23

**Explanatory Guidance on the Belfast Guidelines
on Amnesty and Accountability 25**

INTRODUCTION 25

PART A. GENERAL PRINCIPLES 29

Guideline 1. Balancing States' Multiple Obligations
and Objectives in Protecting Human Rights 29

Guideline 2. Accountability 31

Guideline 3. The Role of Prosecutions 32

Guideline 4. The Role of Amnesties 33

Guideline 5. Linking Amnesty with Accountability 34

PART B: SCOPE OF AMNESTIES 36

Guideline 6. Amnesties and the International Obligations to Prosecute 36

Guideline 7. Eligible Offences 45

Guideline 8. Eligible Offenders 46

Guideline 9. Temporal Scope 49

Guideline 10. Geographic Scope 50

PART C. AMNESTY CONDITIONS 45

Guideline 11. Prior Conditions on Amnesty Beneficiaries 51

Guideline 12. Conditions of Future Conduct on Amnesty Beneficiaries 53

PART D. AMNESTY ADOPTION, IMPLEMENTATION AND REVIEW 56

Guideline 13. Adherence to Domestic Law 56

Guideline 14. Method of Enactment and Public Consultation 56

Guideline 15. Legal Effects 58

Guideline 16. Administering the Amnesty 60

Guideline 17. Annulling Amnesties 61

Guideline 18. International Courts and National Amnesties 62

CONCLUSION 63

The Belfast Guidelines on Amnesty and Accountability

INTRODUCTION

Aims of the Guidelines

The Belfast Guidelines on Amnesty and Accountability aim to assist all those seeking to make or evaluate decisions on amnesties and accountability in the midst or in the wake of conflict or repression. The Guidelines:

- identify the multiple obligations and objectives facing states in protecting human rights

- explain the legal status of amnesties within the framework of the multiple legal obligations that states must reconcile

- assist states in recognising the positive role of certain forms of amnesty in advancing transitional policy and conflict transformation goals

- present ways that amnesties and any associated processes or institutions can be designed to complement accountability

- recommend approaches that allow public participation and independent review of decisions to enact and grant amnesty

The Guidelines are divided into four parts: general principles; scope of amnesty; amnesty conditions; and amnesty adoption, implementation and review. All guidelines should be interpreted in accordance with the General Principles in Part A.

Expert Group Composition

The Belfast Guidelines were drafted by an Expert Group of internationally respected human rights and conflict resolution scholars and practitioners. Within the necessary constraints of keeping the group to a workable size, participants were identified based on multiple criteria:

- *Geography:* to reflect different world regions and areas in which there is recent experience of dealing with gross violations of human rights

- *Disciplinary/Professional Expertise:* to bring together leading figures in a range of scholarly and practitioner backgrounds, including law, criminology, psychology and political science

- *Approach to Amnesty:* to solicit diverse views on how amnesties can be used in the midst or in the wake of mass atrocities

The members of the Expert Group were:[1]

- Barney Afako, Ugandan lawyer and a legal consultant in peace processes in Uganda and Darfur, Sudan

- Mahnoush H. Arsanjani, Commissioner, Bahrain Independent Commission of Inquiry and former Director of the Codification Division, UN Office of Legal Affairs

- Christine Bell, Professor of Public International Law, Edinburgh University

- Chaloka Beyani, Senior Lecturer in International Law, London School of Economics and UN Special Rapporteur on the Human Rights of Internally Displaced Persons

- Michael Broache, Fellow in the Doctorate Political Science program at Columbia University

- Colm Campbell, Professor of Law, Transitional Justice Institute, University of Ulster

- Mark Freeman, Executive Director, Institute for Integrated Transitions
- Tom Hadden, Emeritus Professor of Law, Queen's University Belfast and Professor of Law, Transitional Justice Institute, University of Ulster
- Brandon Hamber, Professor of Peace and Conflict and Director, International Conflict Research Institute, University of Ulster
- Hurst Hannum, Professor of International Law, Fletcher School of Law and Diplomacy, Tufts University
- David Kretzmer, Emeritus Professor of International Law, Hebrew University of Jerusalem
- Suzannah Linton, Professor of International Law, Bangor Law School
- Kieran McEvoy, Professor of Law and Transitional Justice, Institute of Criminology and Criminal Justice, Queen's University Belfast
- Louise Mallinder, Reader in Human Rights and International Law, Transitional Justice Institute, University of Ulster
- William A. Schabas, Professor of International Law, Middlesex University; and Professor of Human Rights and Chairman, Irish Centre for Human Rights, National University of Ireland Galway
- Ronald C. Slye, Professor of Law, Seattle University School of Law; and a commissioner on the Truth, Justice and Reconciliation Commission, Kenya
- Yasmin Sooka, Executive Director, Foundation for Human Rights, South Africa

- Joe William, Founder Director and Senior Advisor, National Peace Council of Sri Lanka, Former Senior Development Advisor, Program Support Unit in Sri Lanka of the Canadian International Development Agency, and PhD student, School of Social and International Studies, University of Bradford

Members of the Expert Group held workshops during 2011 and 2012. It was agreed at the outset that no member should be entitled to enter a personal dissent or reservation. The Guidelines thus reflect the consensus opinion of the Expert Group.

Before publication, the Guidelines were circulated to practitioners and scholars identified by the project experts as part of a confidential consultation process in an effort to ensure that the Guidelines are responsive to the needs of multiple actors and reflective of diverse views on amnesties.

The Evidence Base

The recommendations adopted in the Guidelines draw on extensive sources and evidence including:

- international treaties and customary international law
- decisions by international criminal courts and human rights bodies
- UN declarations, guidelines, resolutions and other standards
- policy papers of the UN and other international organisations
- national legislation
- national case law
- truth commission reports
- peace agreements

- scholarly writings
- views expressed by the Expert Group
- feedback received during the consultation process

The evidence underpinning each Guideline is briefly reviewed in the accompanying Explanatory Guidance. In addition, the Commentary to the Guidelines will provide a detailed analysis of all relevant evidence.[2] This will inter alia provide specific examples of where states have adopted measures such as those proposed in the Guidelines.

In assessing the legitimacy and legality of various forms of amnesty, the Guidelines refer to the status of amnesties under current formulations of international law. For some aspects of amnesty design, such as providing mechanisms for greater victim participation, no direct international legal standards exist. In such cases, the Guidelines draw on individual case studies and existing research to make policy recommendations.

The Guidelines are not structured as a checklist to determine the acceptability of an amnesty, but rather as elements that can be combined and balanced against each other to effectively craft or reach an evaluation on an amnesty's overall acceptability. Depending on a particular context, some elements contained may be more relevant than others.

A. GENERAL PRINCIPLES

1. **Balancing States' Multiple Obligations and Objectives in Protecting Human Rights**

   a) In responding to mass violence perpetrated during conflict and repression, states have multiple obligations under international law to protect human rights and restore or establish peace and stability. With respect to gross violations of human rights[3] and international crimes, these can include:

   i. the obligation to investigate what happened and who was responsible

   ii. the obligation to prosecute those responsible

   iii. the obligation to provide remedies for victims

   iv. the obligation to prevent the recurrence of the crimes and abuses

   v. the obligation to ensure the effective protection of human rights for the future

   These obligations correspond to victims' rights to truth, justice, reparations and guarantees of non-recurrence. Where multiple obligations are applicable, they often cannot be fulfilled simultaneously or rapidly. International law provides limited guidance on how states should prioritise their fulfilment. States have a positive duty to satisfy each of them as far as possible and should seek to develop complementary mechanisms rather than fulfilling one legal obligation while neglecting others.

   b) In seeking to fulfil these obligations, states may be guided by broader policy objectives, which can include:

   i. ending the conflict or repression

ii. restoring public order and stability

iii. establishing democratic structures and the rule of law

iv. dealing with the underlying causes of the conflict or repression

v. promoting reconciliation, sustainable peace and other similar objectives

Like the obligations listed above, these policy objectives often cannot be achieved simultaneously or rapidly and therefore may need to be balanced against each other and against the state's obligations.

c) Amnesties can be designed to further a state's compliance with its legal obligations while also meeting its broader policy objectives.

2. Accountability

Those responsible for gross violations of human rights or international crimes should be held accountable. In addition to legal mechanisms of accountability, which normally give rise to individual prosecution, there are non-legal mechanisms the use of which may, in some contexts, be preferable. Key elements of an effective accountability process include:

a) investigating and identifying individuals or institutions that can be held to account for their decisions, actions or omissions

b) holding these individuals or institutions to account through a process in which they are to disclose and explain their actions

c) subjecting such individuals or institutions to a process through which sanctions can be imposed on individuals and reforms imposed on relevant institutions. Appropriate sanctions may include imprisonment, exclusion from public office, limitations of civil and political rights, requirements to apologise, and requirements to contribute to material or symbolic reparations for victims

As discussed in Guideline 5, depending on how they are framed and implemented, amnesties can contribute to accountability.

3. The Role of Prosecutions

a) International law creates obligations on states to prosecute and punish international crimes (see Guideline 6), and equivalent offences are often criminalised in domestic law. Prosecution can serve to strengthen the condemnation of these crimes. It may also contribute to a number of other legitimate objectives such as deterrence, retribution, rehabilitation and reconciliation.

b) After extensive gross human rights violations or violent conflict within a society, there are often substantial legal, political, economic, and social challenges to pursuing widespread prosecutions. It is rarely possible or practical to prosecute all offenders.

c) In practice, all legal systems, including international criminal law, allow for some prosecutorial discretion in deciding which suspects or which incidents to select and prioritise for prosecution. In some, prosecutors have discretion to forego prosecution if it would not be in the public interest. Where prosecution strategies are developed to select and prioritise crimes that will be investigated, decisions will be made not to prosecute other offences, or to delay those prosecutions until crimes deemed to be of a higher priority have been processed. Where mass atrocities are perpetrated, the unselected or deprioritised cases may include serious crimes.

d) As discussed in Guideline 5, carefully designed amnesties combined with selective prosecution strategies can be consistent with a state's international obligations and can further the legitimate objectives of a state responding to widespread criminal acts. Depending on their design and implementation, amnesties may also directly facilitate objectives traditionally associated with prosecution, including deterrence (where amnesty is conditional on disarmament and non-recidivism) and stigmatisation (where amnesty is conditional on public confession).

4. **The Role of Amnesties**

a) Amnesties are used for a wide range of purposes during ongoing conflicts and repression or as part of political transitions. At different stages, positive objectives of amnesties can include:

   i. encouraging combatants to surrender and disarm

   ii. persuading authoritarian rulers to hand over power

   iii. building trust between warring factions

   iv. facilitating peace agreements

   v. releasing political prisoners

   vi. encouraging exiles to return

   vii. providing an incentive to offenders to participate in truth recovery or reconciliation programmes

b) In all contexts, where amnesties cover serious crimes, it is important to distinguish between illegitimate and legitimate amnesties. Illegitimate amnesties are generally unconditional and have the effect of preventing investigations and ensuring impunity for persons responsible for serious crimes. Amnesties are more likely to be viewed as legitimate where they are primarily designed to create institutional and security conditions for the sustainable protection of human rights, and require individual offenders to engage with measures to ensure truth, accountability and reparations.

5. Linking Amnesty with Accountability

Amnesties can be designed to complement or operate sequentially with judicial and non-judicial accountability processes in a way that furthers a state's multiple obligations and objectives. Such combined approaches can:

a) deliver some form of truth and accountability for cases which are not selected for prosecution

b) focus limited prosecutorial resources on those cases which are deemed to be of a higher priority or where the perpetrator has failed to fulfil the conditions of the amnesty

c) contribute to a broader range of conflict transformation goals than an exclusive focus on prosecutions (see Guideline 4)

d) deliver greater consistency with a state's international obligations than broad amnesties that prevent all prosecutions

B. SCOPE OF AMNESTIES

6. Amnesties and International Obligations to Prosecute

a) Accountability should be pursued for international crimes and gross violations of human rights but international law allows states some flexibility and discretion with respect to considering amnesties.

b) No international treaty explicitly prohibits amnesties. Article 6(5) of Additional Protocol II to the Geneva Conventions, which relates to non-international armed conflicts, encourages states to enact amnesties at the end of hostilities. As a result, the status of amnesties under international law is generally evaluated for incompatibility with treaties prohibiting specific crimes, with interpretations of customary international law, and with the obligation to provide a remedy under international human rights law.

c) International crimes, such as genocide, grave breaches of the Geneva Conventions, torture and enforced disappearances, are today generally prohibited by treaty. These treaties require states parties to enact domestic legislation to provide effective penalties for these crimes. The Geneva Conventions of 1949 also require states parties to search for persons alleged to have perpetrated grave breaches with the goal of bringing them to trial. The conventions on torture and enforced disappearances require states parties to submit cases to their competent authorities for the purpose of prosecution, but these treaties also stipulate that the authorities shall decide whether to prosecute in a similar manner as they would for ordinary offences of a serious nature. In making these decisions, national criminal justice systems can apply established principles of law, for example, by exercising discretion in developing selective prosecution strategies. Selective prosecution strategies are also employed by international and hybrid courts. As a result, states will not necessarily be violating their obligations if, due to the exercise of prosecutorial discretion, they do not prosecute all perpetrators or instances of these crimes. Decisions to select or prioritise cases should be made on the basis of transparent and objective criteria. As indicated in Guideline 5, carefully designed amnesties can complement selective prosecution strategies.

d) Crimes against humanity and war crimes committed in non-international armed conflicts have been defined in the Rome Statute of the International Criminal Court (ICC) and where it has jurisdiction, the ICC can prosecute these crimes. These developments together with the case law of international courts and the opinions of authoritative bodies have provided greater clarity on the nature of these offences and contributed to a body of opinion to support the existence of a customary prohibition on amnesties for international crimes. However, other sources of *opinio juris* from domestic and hybrid courts together with state practice on amnesties does not reflect an established, explicit and categorical customary prohibition of amnesties for international crimes.

e) Within international human rights law, there are differences in the approach of the regional human rights courts on whether there is an obligation to prosecute gross violations of human rights or whether it is sufficient that states investigate such violations and provide remedies for those affected. Amnesties enacted in different regions of the world may be subject to different standards.

7. Eligible Offences

a) The criteria for determining which acts qualify for amnesty should be clearly specified and limited in scope to minimise the potential for conflict with any applicable obligation to prosecute under international criminal law or international human rights law. Finding a balance between limiting the crimes covered by the amnesty and fulfilling the amnesty's objectives can be challenging. For example, excluding war crimes may deter many combatants from surrendering, if they are unsure whether their conflict-related actions constitute war crimes.

b) Limitations to the scope of eligible offences in an amnesty can be made in several ways, including:

i. explicitly listing offences that are excluded from the scope of the amnesty

   ii. granting amnesty for a non-exhaustive list of conflict-related or political offences but with guidelines on how to distinguish political from ordinary offences

   iii. granting amnesty for an exhaustive list of offences

   Where an amnesty is restricted to political or conflict-related offenses or where specific offenses are excluded from the amnesty, perpetrators of ordinary offenses and excluded crimes will remain liable for prosecution. When an offender has committed both included and excluded offenses, a partial amnesty could be possible. As noted in Guideline 16, the implementation of limited amnesties requires individual determinations of their application.

c) Subject to a state's multiple obligations, the exclusion of the following acts from an amnesty may serve to increase its legitimacy and legality:

   i. serious international crimes

   ii. other serious acts of violence against persons that may not rise to the level of an international crime

   iii. acts or offences motivated by personal gain or malice

   As set out in Guideline 8, these restrictions on the acts and offences excluded from an amnesty can be combined with restrictions on the scope of eligible beneficiaries.

8. Eligible Beneficiaries

a) The purpose of each amnesty and the political circumstances within the state will determine which persons an amnesty should exclude or include. Domestic and international law will also regulate the choice of beneficiaries.

b) An amnesty should set forth clearly the criteria for determining which offenders may be eligible for amnesty, which categories of offenders are excluded from the amnesty, or both. Distinctions can be made on the basis of

   i. allegiance or membership in a particular state institution or non-state body

   ii. rank within the institution or body, or perceived level of responsibility therein

c) Amnesties that distinguish between beneficiaries on the basis of their affiliation should take into account any differences in the liabilities of persons affiliated with state institutions and those who are not under domestic law. These differences can result from, for example, domestic regulations on the use of force and pre-existing amnesties, immunities or indemnities. The different liabilities created for different categories of offenders under international law should also be taken into account. For example, international human rights law generally applies only to the actions of states and some international conventions, such as the Convention Against Torture, are applicable only to state agents. Applying such distinctions, however, may undercut efforts to foster reconciliation among former antagonists.

d) Amnesties that distinguish in respect of rank may exclude military and political leaders while making amnesty available to lower-level offenders. Such distinctions balance amnesty with accountability, but can be problematic where high-ranking individuals are key stakeholders in a political transition. Amnesties that exclude high-ranking individuals may draw upon the principle of command responsibility found in international criminal law, and the prosecutorial strategies of international and hybrid courts that focus on those who are "most responsible".

e) Under international criminal law, subordinates are liable for international crimes that they commit when following the orders of a superior, but they can be relieved of this liability where they were under a legal obligation to obey superior orders, where they did not know that the order was unlawful and where the order was not manifestly unlawful. For all levels of offenders grounds for excluding criminal liability include substantially diminished mental capacity and duress. In addition, mitigating factors such as efforts made by the convicted person to compensate victims and to cooperate with judicial authorities, and the age, education, social and economic condition of the convicted person can be taken into account at sentencing. The principles that provide for such mitigation or relief of liability could be incorporated into an amnesty. Where lower-level offenders are granted amnesty, as explored in Guideline 11, the amnesty can be made conditional on their participation in non-judicial accountability processes.

f) Special attention should be paid in amnesties to the treatment of children responsible for acts that may qualify as national or international crimes. International law and most domestic legal systems provide for a minimum age of criminal responsibility. Where an individual is below this age at the time of the offence and thus is not criminally responsible, *a fortiori* he or she need not be included within the scope of an amnesty. Where access to demobilisation and reintegration programmes is dependent on participation in an amnesty process, care should be taken to address the needs of children who do not fall within the amnesty because of their lack of legal criminal responsibility. Children who are above the minimum age of criminal responsibility but below 18 years at the time of their offences may be liable for criminal prosecution. They may therefore be included within amnesty processes, and care should then be taken to address their particular needs and experiences.

9. Temporal Scope

a) To avoid ambiguity, amnesties should state the start and end dates within which eligible crimes must have been committed. The period between the start and end dates should be the minimum necessary for the achievement of the law's objectives. The selection of these dates can affect the legitimacy of the amnesty (e.g., where the cut-off dates are used strategically to exclude particular notorious events or crimes committed by only one faction, or where the start date of a conflict is the subject of contestation).

b) The crime of enforced disappearances has been characterised as a continuous crime in international treaties and in the case law of some domestic and international courts. Since the crime is deemed to continue until the fate of the disappeared person has been clarified, amnesties should not bar investigations regardless of when the disappearance occurred.

10. Geographic Scope

Where a conflict or policy of state repression primarily affected one region of a country, the amnesty may be limited to crimes committed within that region. Such limitations minimise the impunity granted but can risk treating victims within and outside the affected region differently. If an amnesty does not address geographic scope, it is generally presumed to apply to the entire country. It may also apply to offences committed by nationals outside the country, but as discussed in Guideline 18, such amnesties cannot bar the state where the crimes were committed from exercising jurisdiction.

C. AMNESTY CONDITIONS

11. Prior Conditions on Amnesty Beneficiaries

Individual offenders may be required to fulfil specified conditions before obtaining amnesty. These conditions may enable an amnesty to contribute to preventing further violence and to facilitate accountability and the fulfilment of victims' rights to truth and reparations. The extent to which offenders will be willing to fulfil such conditions may depend on a range of factors, such as the political and security context; cultural approaches to truth-telling and justice; and the extent to which participation will require acknowledgement or repudiation of their past actions. Imposing a more extensive range of conditions may result in fewer offenders participating, but the inclusion of such conditions may serve to increase an amnesty's legitimacy and legality and further compliance with a state's international obligations to investigate and provide remedies. Where individuals fail to comply fully with applicable conditions, amnesty should be withheld. Preconditions for the conferral of an amnesty may include:

a) submitting individual applications

b) surrendering and participating in disarmament, demobilisation and reintegration programmes

c) participating in traditional or restorative justice processes

d) fully disclosing personal involvement in offences, with penalties for false testimony

e) providing information on third party involvement with respect to offences

f) testifying (publicly or privately) in a truth commission, public inquiry or other truth-recovery process

g) testifying at the trial of those who were not granted or eligible for amnesty

h) surrendering assets illegitimately acquired

i) contributing materially and/or symbolically to reparations

12. Conditions of Future Conduct on Amnesty Beneficiaries

a) To increase the legitimacy and legality of an amnesty, individual beneficiaries may be subject to conditions that they must fulfil in order to avoid revocation of the benefits. Such conditions provide a means for the state to hold accountable individuals who might abuse the amnesty process, and may encourage beneficiaries to contribute to ongoing reconciliation processes. However, uncertainty in whether an amnesty will be made permanent may make it less attractive for some offenders. Conditions that could be imposed for a beneficiary to retain amnesty may include:

   i. not breaching the conditions on which the amnesty was originally granted

   ii. refraining from the commission of new conflict-related or political offences, or any other type of criminal activity

   iii. time-limited bans on owning dangerous weapons, standing for election or public office, and/or serving in the police or armed forces

b) Some of the conditions for amnesty listed under Guideline 11 (c) to (i) may be included as a condition of future conduct, following the conferral of amnesty, rather than as a prior condition.

c) To facilitate the enforcement of conditions of future conduct, an amnesty can grant offenders immunity from prosecution for a limited period of time, after which the grant of immunity would be made permanent if the offender has fulfilled all of the conditions of future conduct, or revoked if such conditions have not been fulfilled. If the individual were to engage in prohibited activity during the applicable period, the temporary immunity could be lifted immediately.

d) To oversee fulfilment of conditions of future conduct, a formal, independent procedure should be established to review or adjudicate compliance. The procedure should specify criteria and rules for determining the level of compliance, and the decision-making body should be appropriately resourced. Where an amnesty is revoked, prosecutions should be pursued for the original crime and any subsequent offences.

D. AMNESTY ADOPTION, IMPLEMENTATION AND REVIEW

13. Adherence to Domestic Law

While all legal systems provide for some form of leniency within their criminal justice processes, granting amnesty during or following conflict or repression may be constrained by domestic law. For an amnesty to be valid under domestic law, at a minimum its enactment must adhere to all relevant formal domestic rules. Where these rules are not respected, national courts should have the independence and authority to declare the amnesty unconstitutional or require amendment of the legislation.

14. Method of Enactment and Public Consultation

a) Amnesties may be enacted through a range of executive and legislative mechanisms, as provided under domestic procedural rules. The mechanism chosen may have implications for the extent to which the amnesty can subsequently be amended or annulled. An amnesty enacted through a constitutional provision will be more difficult to amend.

b) Public consultation in the design of an amnesty may increase its legitimacy. Where appropriate, such consultation should include the involvement of potentially marginalised groups such as victims, women, children, displaced persons, minorities and former combatants. It can take various forms including public meetings, surveys, focus groups and the consideration of written submissions.

c) Some amnesties have been confirmed by national referenda, which can serve to increase their legitimacy. This can entail holding votes on a peace agreement or new constitution that includes amnesty provisions, thus establishing a link to broader efforts to deliver peace and democracy. Alternatively, amnesty can be the sole focus of a referendum to ensure that the vote on amnesty is not commingled with other issues. Where minorities were victimised by a government representing the majority community, it may be desirable to ensure that a positive vote is obtained in each affected community by requiring an enhanced majority.

d) Provision for public participation is one component of amnesty design but is insufficient by itself to guarantee the legitimacy or legality of an amnesty that otherwise violates domestic or international law.

e) "Self-amnesties" are amnesties adopted unilaterally by regimes that are responsible for international crimes or gross violations of human rights, and which often have seized power illegally. Subject to a state's multiple obligations, such amnesties should be regarded as *prima facie* illegal and illegitimate.

15. **Legal Effects**

a) Amnesties may have multiple legal consequences for individual beneficiaries in relation to the designated offences. These can include:

   i. preventing new criminal investigations being opened

   ii. stopping ongoing criminal investigations and trials

   iii. reducing prison sentences

   iv. releasing prisoners

   v. granting pardons

   vi. erasing criminal records

   vii. barring civil liability

b) Where an amnesty bars civil liability, either explicitly in the amnesty legislation or implicitly where access to civil remedies is dependent on prior criminal convictions, administrative reparations programmes should be considered to provide remedies to victims.

c) If an amnesty process has been designed to distinguish between different categories of offenders or crimes, the legal effects of the amnesty may differ between categories of beneficiaries. Offences that are more serious may receive only sentence reductions under the law, while less serious offences may obtain full amnesty. Such a tiered approach can provide an element of proportionality in the legal consequences for different categories of offenders and may thus increase an amnesty's legitimacy or legality.

16. Administering the Amnesty

a) For amnesties with limitations and conditions, a process is needed to determine an individual's eligibility for amnesty. Amnesty implementation processes can be overseen by domestic courts, advisory bodies that report to the government, specially-appointed amnesty commissions, or truth commissions with the power to grant or recommend amnesty. The institution responsible to administer an amnesty should

   i. be independent

   ii. represent diverse social sectors

   iii. have appropriate skills to implement the amnesty

   iv. possess the jurisdiction and legal powers to carry out its mandate effectively

   v. be sufficiently resourced to make initial determinations on amnesty eligibility and, if appropriate, to monitor adherence to conditions over prescribed periods

b) The involvement of victims and affected communities in an amnesty's implementation process generally serves to increase its legitimacy. This could entail allowing affected victims and community members to participate in hearings to determine whether individual applications for amnesty should be approved. To ensure effective participation, it is also important to inform victims in a timely manner of where and when the hearing will take place, to provide or enable legal representation and/or financial support towards travel or other expenses related to attending the hearing, and to ensure effective witness support and protection. Where victims will witness offender testimony in amnesty hearings, care should be taken to avoid the victims' re-traumatisation. Victims should be informed of the final amnesty decision before it is made public.

c) Processes to administer amnesties should take into account the procedural rights of amnesty applicants. In particular, applicants should be able to appeal decisions of the amnesty-implementing body to independent courts.

17. Annulling Amnesties

a) In a few countries, domestic courts or legislatures have annulled long-standing and previously implemented amnesties. To create the possibility of future annulment, an amnesty could make provision for future domestic judicial review. However, the uncertainty created by such provisions may undermine the ability of the amnesty to contribute to achieving greater stability, human rights protections, and reconciliation. Furthermore, where an amnesty is annulled, other obstacles to criminal accountability may endure.

b) Where amnesty legislation explicitly limits the scope of amnesty, but this scope is extended beyond these limits through overly broad case law, the reopening of criminal cases may not require the annulment of the amnesty, but rather the consistent application of any limitations or conditions within the amnesty legislation.

18. International Courts and National Amnesties

a) Although amnesties bar criminal proceedings within the states that enacted the amnesty, they cannot bar international, hybrid or foreign courts from exercising jurisdiction. Such courts may decide under their own jurisdiction whether to recognise an amnesty.

b) Where an international or hybrid criminal tribunal has jurisdiction, a state may be required under its treaty obligations to cooperate with the tribunal. Such cooperation can include surrendering a person who has benefited from amnesty at the national level to stand trial before the international court.

c) International and hybrid criminal tribunals are empowered to convict individuals, but they cannot declare a national amnesty unconstitutional or order a state to annul its amnesty legislation. As a result, even where such tribunals declare an amnesty to be inoperative at the international level in an individual case, it may continue to have effect at the domestic level. In practice this can mean that the majority of offenders within the state granting the amnesty will continue to benefit from the amnesty.

d) Regional human rights courts can consider whether, by granting amnesty, a state over which it has jurisdiction is in violation of its international obligations. Where these courts find a violation, they can recommend a range of remedies, including ordering that the amnesty be annulled. If the state complies with such a ruling, it can result in the amnesty ceasing to have effect in domestic law.

Explanatory Guidance on the Belfast Guidelines on Amnesty and Accountability

Louise Mallinder

1. ABSTRACT

The Belfast Guidelines on Amnesty and Accountability have been developed by an Expert Group of independent, interdisciplinary scholars and practitioners from different world regions and areas with recent experience of dealing with gross human rights violations. The Guidelines aim to assist those seeking to make or evaluate decisions on amnesties and accountability in the midst or wake of conflict or repression. The Guidelines are divided into four parts: general principles, scope of the amnesty, amnesty conditions, and amnesty adoption, implementation and review. This Explanatory Guidance sets out the law, standards and practice that support each Guideline, as well as the discussion that informed the drafting.

2. INTRODUCTION

States have used amnesties for millennia to resolve to armed conflict, to reconcile to the state citizens who breached national laws, and to remedy the injustices created by overly rigid criminal justice processes.[4] In the past, amnesties were regarded as exercises of executive discretion to be regulated by domestic law and generally received international consideration only when they were included in peace agreements between states. The expansion of international law following World War II prompted greater international attention on the status of amnesty laws, which were predominantly viewed favourably. For example, Additional Protocol II to the Geneva Conventions 1977 explicitly encourages states to enact the "broadest possible amnesty" at the end of hostilities.[5] The Commentary on the Additional Protocols notes that this provision is intended "to encourage gestures of reconciliation which can contribute to re-establishing normal relations in the life of a nation which has been divided."[6] The UN Sub-Commission on Prevention of Discrimination and Protection of Minorities emphasised the importance that the promulgation of amnesty laws "could have for the safeguard and promotion of human rights and fundamental freedoms"[7] in its 1983 decision to commission the first comparative study of amnesty laws.[8] The study described the positive role of amnesties as including releasing all political prisoners; encouraging "national consensus in the wake of political change brought about in a democratic framework;" initiating the "first act in the initiation of a democratic process;" and blocking "an internal crisis" or marking "the end of an international armed conflict."[9] This appreciation of the positive contributions of amnesties to peace and democracy frequently prompted organs of the United Nations to call upon war-torn states to enact amnesties.[10]

In contrast, governments wishing to enact amnesties today increasingly face international legal, diplomatic and economic pressure to refrain from amnestying international crimes and gross violations of human rights. This shift is due the expansion of the instruments and institutions of international human rights law, international humanitarian law and international criminal law, and the growth of civil society organisations that monitor compliance with these legal regimes. From the late 1990s, these developments gave rise to a growing body of international case law and other authoritative opinions that gradually found that where amnesties are granted for international crimes or gross violations of human rights they breach obligations of states under international law.[11] Furthermore, it is increasingly argued that rather than protecting human rights, the impunity created by amnesties may embolden "beneficiaries to commit further crimes" and destabilise efforts to achieve sustainable peace.[12]

Despite these developments, states have declined proposals to include explicit prohibitions on amnesties in international treaties.[13] Furthermore, amnesties for international crimes and gross violations of human rights continue to be enacted, and in some cases, receive international support and are endorsed by national courts.[14] As discussed in Guideline 6, this supports arguments that international law allows states some flexibility and discretion with respect to considering amnesties. The development of international law and practice is however influencing the *shape* and *role* of amnesties as today amnesties are rarely granted unconditionally to war criminals and human rights abusers. Instead, amnesties are now often conditioned on individual offenders engaging with processes to prevent further violence and deliver accountability, and are designed to complement selective prosecution strategies. In such contexts, amnesty can be used strategically to enhance the state's fulfilment with its multiple legal obligations.

Assertions of the impact of amnesties on the protection of human rights generally treat amnesties as uniform phenomena and do not take these changes in their conditionality into account. Nonetheless, recent research into the impacts of amnesties has found that there is a lack of evidence that amnesties impede human rights protections. For example, analyses of amnesties in individual states, such as Spain and Mozambique,[15] reveal that even amnesties for serious crimes can form part of transitions to stable democracy and reduced human rights violations. These examples provide a basis to argue that, at a minimum, it has not been proven that amnesties are inherently harmful for peace or other transitional goals. Recognising that amnesties do not always impede the protection of human rights does not mean that their use enhances human rights protections or that better outcomes would have been obtained if amnesty had not been used. Causal arguments that amnesties can enhance human rights protections are hard to prove as not all amnesties seek to do this. In addition, even where the existence of amnesties correlates to improvements in human rights, this is not proof that the amnesty itself was the cause of those improvements.[16] In recent years, large-scale, quantitative, comparative studies have sought to measure the impact of transitional justice processes including amnesties on improving human rights and achieving democracy. For example, Olsen, Payne and Reiter found that where trials or amnesties were implemented in the absence of other transitional justice mechanisms, neither proved to "have a statistically significant effect in improving human rights and democracy."[17] In contrast, where transitional states used both trials and amnesty the combination produced "stronger democracies and human rights records."[18] Such combinations could be achieved through processes of selective prosecutions accompanied by limited amnesties, or by sequencing trials and amnesty. Olsen et al further contend that where truth commissions also form part of a transitional process, the likelihood of positive outcomes is even higher.[19] Similar arguments were made by Ricci who based on quantitative analysis found that countries which utilised a combination of amnesties and trials "were more likely to have a higher peace sustainability than countries which only utilised one mechanism."[20] These studies suggest that amnesties if adopted with other transitional justice mechanisms may enhance human rights protections, which provides empirical support for the approach taken in the Guidelines that as far as possible amnesties should be designed to complement mechanisms to deliver accountability and truth.

Recognition of the continued flexibility of international law on the status of amnesties and concerns about how an absolute prohibition on amnesties could affect the protection of human rights in countries faced with or transitioning from conflict and repression led to the proposal for the production by a group of independent, interdisciplinary scholars and practitioners from different world regions of a set of guidelines for those seeking to make or evaluate decisions on amnesties and accountability in the midst or wake of conflict or repression.

The Guidelines draw on international legal sources, such as international treaties and customary international law; decisions by international criminal courts and human rights bodies; UN declarations, guidelines, resolutions and other standards; as well as individual case studies;[21] and existing research. This Explanatory Guidance sets out the law, standards and practice that support each Guideline, as well as the discussion that informed the drafting.

3. GENERAL PRINCIPLES

Guideline 1. Balancing States' Multiple Obligations and Objectives in Protecting Human Rights

Determinations of the legality of amnesties often focus on whether they conflict with the state's duty to prosecute. However, international crimes and gross violations of human rights create multiple international legal obligations for states, which can all affect the legality of an amnesty. These include the obligations to investigate, prosecute, provide remedies for victims, prevent the recurrence of the crimes and abuses, and ensure the effective protection of human rights for the future. Guideline 1(a) draws attention to all these legal obligations and explores their implications for the legality of amnesties. This should be read alongside Guideline 6 that explores the parameters of the duty to prosecute and Guideline 11 that discusses how the conditionality of an amnesty can affect its legality and legitimacy.

It is widely accepted that the human rights obligations of states should be treated as "indivisible, interdependent, interrelated and of course of equal importance to human dignity."[22] However, in practice, conflicted and transitional states may face many challenges in fulfilling their obligations (see Guideline 3) and these obligations may come into tension with one another. For example, amnesties can limit fulfilment of a state's obligation to prosecute in order to fulfil other obligations, such as preventing further human rights violations. Where amnesties cause conflict between a state's competing legal obligations there is no binding law to indicate how states should resolve any incompatibilities.[23] However, the International Law Commission (ILC) recommends that lawyers seek to harmonise between competing legal standards.[24] It defined harmonisation as "a generally accepted principle that when several norms bear on a single issue they should, to the extent possible, be interpreted so as to give rise to a single set of compatible obligations."[25] Such processes of harmonisation may require competing obligations to be balanced against one another with the result that some obligations are "limited or tempered" by other obligations.[26] The case law of international tribunals and human rights monitoring bodies also notes human rights obligations are not absolute and emphasises the importance of balancing competing obligations, even in relation to prosecutions for serious crimes. For example, a concurring opinion by the president of the Inter-American Court of Human Rights supported by four other judges in the *El Mozote v El Salvador* case acknowledged the importance of balancing the right of victims to peace against the duty to prosecute gross human rights violations. This opinion argued "none of those rights and obligations is of an absolute nature, it is legitimate that they be weighed in such a way that the satisfaction of some does not affect the exercise of the others disproportionately."[27] Where amnesties create conflicts between states' legal obligations, Guideline 1(a) recommends that harmonisation be pursued with the overall aim of protecting human rights and fulfilling the full range of states' obligations to the greatest extent possible.

Policy objectives as well as legal obligations shape the design of amnesties and other transitional justice processes. Guideline 1(b) provides examples of relevant policy objectives, and notes that although the fulfilment of all these objectives is desirable, this often cannot be achieved simultaneously or rapidly. It therefore recommends that these objectives may need to be balanced against each other and against states' obligations.

Guideline 2. Accountability

Accountability has emerged as a core principle of efforts to deal with legacies of international crimes and gross violations of human rights and Guideline 2 affirms the importance of holding perpetrators to account.[28] For lawyers, accountability generally entails individual or state accountability before (quasi-)judicial institutions.[29] Guideline 2 draws upon interdisciplinary social scientific approaches,[30] which generally envisage broader forms of accountability that seek to hold not just individuals, but also institutions, corporations and other entities responsible for their actions; that can be delivered by processes outside formal legal institutions; and that seek to contribute to a broader range of social goals than those classically ascribed to criminal prosecutions. The affirmation in Guideline 2, which is restated in Guideline 6, that those responsible for international crimes and gross violations of human rights should be held to account draws on legal standards as well as social scientific analyses on the importance of accountability.

Drawing on this interdisciplinary literature, Guideline 2 identifies key elements of effective accountability processes. Transitional justice mechanisms can deliver these elements to differing degrees. For example, criminal prosecutions can deliver the enforcement dimension of individual accountability through conviction and sentencing, but may create incentives for offenders to obfuscate rather than answer for their actions.[31] Non-judicial accountability mechanisms, such as truth commissions, public inquiries, parliamentary committees, ombudsmen or human rights commissions, vetting programmes and restorative or traditional justice mechanisms can identify those persons to be held accountable, require offenders to acknowledge and explain their actions or omissions, and impose a range of sanctions. These processes can reveal truths that may not otherwise be available and reveal wider patterns of abuse or structural injustice. As noted in Guideline 15, the sanctions imposed on individual offenders could be designed to distinguish the gravity of the offence or their level of culpability.

Although amnesties are designed to restrict prosecutions, as discussed in Guideline 5, limited amnesties can complement selective prosecution strategies. In addition, amnesties do not necessarily block the operations of non-prosecutorial accountability mechanisms, and as noted in Guidelines 5, 10 and 11, individual grants of amnesty can be conditioned on participation in accountability processes. As a result, Guideline 2 concludes by stating that amnesties can contribute to accountability.

Guideline 3. The Role of Prosecutions

Guideline 3(a) emphasises the importance of prosecutions for international crimes and other serious offences and notes that they can contribute to the fulfilment of a range of objectives, including deterrence, retribution, rehabilitation, expression of the values of the rule of law, and reconciliation. However, after widespread criminality, it is not always either possible or practical to prosecute all offenders due to legal, political and social challenges. The range of challenges listed in paragraph (b) makes clear why, as acknowledged by the UN Secretary General, "[i]n the end, in post-conflict countries, the vast majority of perpetrators of serious violations … will never be tried, whether internationally or domestically."[32] To address this "impunity gap," the UN Secretary-General suggested that prosecutors should develop prosecutorial policies that are "strategic, based on clear criteria, and take account of the social context."[33] This approach is adopted in paragraph (c) which draws on the implications of such strategies on prosecutions for widespread human rights violations and suggests that some prosecutorial selectivity as implemented in national criminal justice systems, the international criminal tribunals and hybrid courts may be appropriate.[34] Experiences show that selective prosecution strategies may result in only some offenders being indicted, with others benefitting from amnesty. For example, the hybrid courts of Cambodia and Sierra Leone only indicted small proportion of each nation's offenders (five[35] and 13[36] respectively), which left thousands of other offenders to benefit from amnesty. Paragraph (d) concludes by noting that amnesties combined with selective prosecution strategies can be consistent with a state's international obligations and may directly facilitate objectives traditionally associated with prosecution.[37]

Guideline 4. The Role of Amnesties

Guideline 4(a) illustrates how amnesties can be enacted for a range of positive objectives. Although the objectives underlying an amnesty are rarely fully transparent, acknowledging these differences is important as objectives can shape the scope of the amnesty, which in turn can affect its legality and legitimacy. The Guidelines here and elsewhere use "legitimacy" as a condition for policies and decisions relating to amnesty as the drafters felt that legitimacy is a broader concept than legality. Legitimacy was viewed as relating to the extent to which inter alia amnesties are created through democratic and participative processes (see Guideline 14), individuals and communities engage with amnesties (see Guideline 16), and amnesties form part of holistic strategies for peace, justice and reconciliation. Legitimacy is viewed as a key component of amnesties achieving positive outcomes.

Guideline 4(b) seeks to distinguish between legitimate and illegitimate amnesties. In doing so, in accordance with the balancing approach of the Guidelines as a whole, the distinction is not drawn solely based on the duty to prosecute, but instead takes into account the extent to which amnesty is designed to facilitate or impede the fulfilment of the states' international obligations and policy objectives. Where amnesties seek to fulfil multiple obligations as far as possible they are more likely to be viewed as legitimate whereas amnesties that aim to achieve impunity without much regard to the duty to prosecute, nor a state's other international obligations, are more likely to be viewed as illegitimate. This approach clearly distinguishes conditional amnesties recommended in Guidelines 11 and 12 from unconditional amnesties (sometimes known as "blanket" amnesties), and it should be read in conjunction with the rejection of self-amnesties in Guideline 14(e). Guideline 4(b) suggests that amnesties are more likely to be viewed as legitimate by domestic and international actors where they are designed to support efforts to protect human rights through measures to reduce violent conflict, to ensure the stability of the transition, to undo past human rights violations, and to promote cooperation by individual offenders with truth, accountability and reconciliation programmes. Examples of international support for such amnesties can be found in the policies of international organisations. For example, the UN Secretary-General has noted that "carefully crafted amnesties can help in the return and reintegration" of former combatants,[38] as the offer of amnesty is believed to encourage more combatants to participate in Disarmament, Demobilisation and Reintegration (DDR) programmes by reassuring them they will not be charged with criminal offences if they surrender. In addition, the use of amnesties to encourage exiles and refugees to return to their country of origin has been supported in the policy documents of the UN High Commission for Refugees.[39]

Guideline 5. Linking Amnesty with Accountability

In general, states do not face an either/or choice between judicial and non-judicial forms of accountability. Instead, multiple mechanisms can be designed to be *complementary*, that is to operate simultaneously at different levels (international, national, or local) or to achieve distinct goals. They can also be *sequenced* to conduct their functions in a particular order. The determination of this order could be due to the political conditions or the ability of one process to feed into the work of another. For example, the findings of a truth recovery process could subsequently be used as evidence in criminal proceedings. Amnesties can complement criminal prosecutions where they are designed in a manner that allows prosecutions to remain possible for crimes (see Guideline 6) or offenders (see Guideline 8) that are excluded from the amnesties' scope, or for offenders who fail to fulfil the amnesties' conditions (see Guideline 11). Guideline 5 lists some ways in which these complementary processes can be beneficial.

In its 2011 amnesty decision in the Ieng Sary case, the Trial Chamber of the Extraordinary Chambers of the Courts of Cambodia noted, "[c]ertain conditional amnesties such as those providing for some form of accountability have also met widespread approval, such as in the case of South Africa, where amnesties were granted as part of the reconciliation process."[40] It continued that "[s]uch amnesties have generally not been invalidated, but rather, applied on a case-by-case basis, depending on a number of factors, including the process by which the amnesty was enacted, the substance and scope of the amnesty, and whether it provided for any alternative form of accountability."[41] The Chamber concluded that amnesties for international crimes "*especially when unaccompanied by any form of accountability* are incompatible with the goals" (emphasis added) of holding perpetrators accountable and providing victims with an effective remedy.[42] This suggests that where an amnesty is accompanied by some form of accountability, courts may take this into account. Guideline 5 takes a similar approach by advocating that as far as possible, amnesties should be made conditional on individual offenders participating in processes that seek to ensure accountability through judicial and non-judicial mechanisms.

4. SCOPE OF AMNESTIES

Guideline 6. Amnesties and the International Obligations to Prosecute

Guideline 6 addresses the most controversial issue with respect to the legality and legitimacy of amnesties. In considering the duty to prosecute, the drafters sought to identify the scope of existing legal standards and to highlight where the law remains unsettled. Due to the contested nature of the duty to prosecute, Guideline 6 sets out to highlight areas in which states retain flexibility in determining their approach to amnesties. The drafters, however, declined to be prescriptive as the legal obligations relating to a national amnesty may depend on numerous factors, such as, when the crimes were committed, the nature of those offences, if and when the state has become a party to relevant treaties, and whether state is subject to the jurisdiction of international courts.

Paragraph (b) notes that no international convention explicitly prohibits amnesty laws. Indeed, when the possibility of incorporating an amnesty prohibition was debated during the negotiations on the Rome Statute of the International Criminal Court 1998[43] and the International Convention for the Protection of All Persons from Enforced Disappearance 2006,[44] it proved so divisive among the negotiating states that the resulting treaties omit any mention of amnesties. To date, as discussed further below, the only explicit treaty reference to amnesties, in Article 6(5) of Additional Protocol II to the Geneva Conventions, which relates to non-international armed conflicts, *encourages* states to "grant the broadest possible amnesty to persons who have participated in the armed conflict" at the end of hostilities.[45]

The absence of a prohibition has meant that the extent to which amnesties come into conflict with international obligations to prosecute is generally evaluated based on composite readings of three distinct international legal regimes: international humanitarian law, international human rights law and international criminal law.[46] This requires engagement with distinct sources of international law, including international treaties, customary international law and international jurisprudence. The Guidelines take a broad approach by referring to the duty to prosecute genocide, serious breaches of humanitarian law in international and internal conflicts, torture and forced disappearances as well as gross violations of human rights. However, to reflect the distinct regimes and sources that underpin the duty to prosecute, the Guidelines declined to articulate a uniform duty to prosecute applicable to these different crimes and violations, and instead, to ensure clarity and accuracy, they are analysed separately within Guideline 6.[47]

Amnesties and Crimes Prohibited by International Treaty

Paragraph (c) reviews the obligation to prosecute created by treaties on genocide,[48] "grave breaches" of the Geneva Conventions,[49] torture,[50] and enforced disappearances.[51] It draws in particular on the wording of the conventions against torture and enforced disappearances, which state that decisions to prosecute those crimes should be taken by national prosecuting authorities "in the same manner as in the case of any ordinary offence of a serious nature under the law of that State Party."[52] In line with the discussion of selective prosecutions in Guideline 3, this paragraph notes that national prosecuting authorities could rely on established discretionary rules, which may in some instances result in a decision not to prosecute. This paragraph concludes by suggesting that even where treaties create an obligation to prosecute, states will not necessarily be violating their obligations if, due to the exercise of prosecutorial discretion, they do not prosecute all perpetrators or instances of these crimes. Decisions to select or prioritise cases should be made based on transparent and objective criteria.

Amnesties and Customary International Law

Paragraph (c) of Guideline 6 addresses the most unsettled area of international law on amnesties, namely the extent to which amnesties for international crimes are prohibited under customary international law. This is particularly significant for crimes against humanity and war crimes committed in non-international armed conflicts as the obligations on states with respect to these crimes are primarily subject to customary international law.

According to the International Court of Justice Statute, customary international law is derived from state practice (ie actions or omissions by states) and *opinio juris* (ie the state practice must be motivated by a belief in the existence of a legal obligation),[53] and the evidence for both will be reviewed in this section. The case law of international courts and the opinions of authoritative bodies have contributed to an extensive body of opinion supporting the existence of a customary duty to prosecute international crimes. However, the drafters were conscious that even if this duty is found to exist, it does not necessarily mean that the duty is absolute and that it precludes the use of amnesties in all instances. As paragraph (c) relates to the existence of a customary prohibition of amnesties, rather than a customary duty to prosecute per se, this section will focus primarily on sources that relate directly to the status of amnesties under customary international law.

Through their statutes and case law, the international tribunals and hybrid courts have defined and prosecuted crimes against humanity and war crimes committed in non-international armed conflicts. In doing so, they pronounced on the duty to prosecute of these crimes under customary international law. In a few cases, they have also expressed views on whether customary prohibitions on amnesties exist. For example, the International Criminal Tribunal on the Former Yugoslavia has considered hypothetical (or alleged) amnesties for international offences in two cases and found that they are prohibited under customary international law.[54] However, these decisions did not cite any state practice to support the court's position. When the hybrid courts in Sierra Leone and Cambodia were asked to consider the status of existing amnesties, they reached different conclusions to the ICTY. For example, the Appeals Chamber of the Special Court of Sierra Leone which, adopting the position of proposed by Antonio Cassese, asserted that "there is not yet any general obligation for states to refrain from amnesty for" crimes against humanity and that "if a state passes any such law, it does not breach a customary rule."[55] More recently, the Trial Chamber of the Extraordinary Chamber of the Courts of Cambodia, which conducted the most extensive review of state practice of any international(ised) criminal court, found that "state practice in relation to other serious international crimes [not prohibited by treaty] is arguably insufficiently uniform to establish an absolute prohibition in relation to them."[56] It follows that even among the international and hybrid courts, there are divergent positions on the existence of a prohibition on amnesty for international crimes under customary international law. Article 38(1)(d) of the International Court of Justice Statute provides that judicial decisions are a "subsidiary means for the determination of rules of law."[57] These decisions are not in themselves sources of law, but rather *opinio juris* on the existence of rules derived from treaty law or customary international law.

The existence of a customary prohibition on amnesties for international crimes has proclaimed in a number of "soft" law instruments.[58] "Soft" law instruments are non-binding on states, and their purpose is generally thought to be to promote "norms" which are believed to be positive and are therefore to be encouraged to have general application.[59] However, as with the decisions of international and hybrid courts, soft law instruments "may be evidence of existing law, or formative of the *opinio juris* or state practice that generates new customary law."[60]

In addition to international case law and soft law standards, other sources of state practice and *opinio juris* that should be considered include the existence or absence of relevant domestic legislation (either granting amnesties for international crimes or requiring prosecutions); state practice in negotiating peace agreements that include or exclude amnesty provisions or in giving diplomatic or financial support to or rejecting amnesty processes; state willingness to include provisions prohibiting amnesty in international conventions; and judgments of domestic courts on the legality of amnesties. Many of these sources undermine the alleged existence of a prohibition on amnesties under customary international law.

State practice on the duty to prosecute has been relied upon by the International Committee of the Red Cross (ICRC) to reinterpret customary international law relating to the duty to prosecute war crimes committed in non-international armed conflicts. The treaty law governing violence against civilians and combatants who are *hors de combat* during internal conflicts, namely Common Article 3 to the Geneva Conventions and Additional Protocol II, creates minimum standards of protection for civilians but contains no duty to prosecute.[61] However, in a 2005 study, the ICRC reinterpreted these provisions in light of its views on customary international humanitarian law proclaiming that "serious violations of international humanitarian law constitute war crimes" regardless of whether they are perpetrated in international or non-international armed conflicts.[62] On this basis, the ICRC has reformulated article 6(5) of Additional Protocol II stating that based on customary law it should now be read as:

> At the end of hostilities, the authorities in power must endeavour to grant the broadest possible amnesty to persons who have participated in a non-international armed conflict, or those deprived of their liberty for reasons related to the armed conflict, *with the exception of persons suspected of, accused of or sentenced for war crimes.* (Emphasis added).[63]

It further stated that amnesties for serious violations of international humanitarian law would be incompatible with the customary rule it had identified "obliging States to investigate and prosecute persons suspected of having committed war crimes in non-international armed conflicts."[64]

The ICRC study based its reinterpretations of Article 6(5) and Common Article 3 on a review of practice. For example, in justifying its more restrictive position on amnesties, the ICRC asserted, "[m]ost amnesties specifically exclude from their scope persons who are suspected of having committed war crimes or other crimes specifically listed under international law."[65] The practice cited by the ICRC study underpinning its position included inter alia five international treaties (including Additional Protocol II), six peace agreements from internal conflicts and national legislation from sixteen states. However, the majority of the peace agreements and over half of the national laws cited provided amnesties for international crimes and gross human rights violations.[66] The limited evidence cited therefore seems to contradict the ICRC's justification for reformulating Article 6(5).

State practice in enacting amnesty laws has also been reviewed in the Amnesty Law Database created by the author. This database, which contains information on over 530 amnesties enacted between 1945 and 2011, reviews inter alia whether an amnesty included or excluded crimes under international law (defined as genocide, crimes against humanity, war crimes, torture or enforced disappearances).[67] It reveals that although from the early 1990s, international crimes began to be excluded more frequently from amnesty legislation, amnesties continue to be granted for these crimes and that from the late 1990s there has been little difference in the numbers of new amnesties that include or exclude international crimes.[68]

In addition to state practice in enacting amnesties, it is also important to consider state practice in encouraging or condemning amnesties in other jurisdictions. There have been amnesties for international crimes have received condemnation in UN Security Council resolutions, the opinions of human rights institutions and statements by some states. However, data gathered in the Amnesty Law Database relating to amnesties enacted for international crimes between 1980 and 2007[69] indicates that international actors, including states, intergovernmental institutions and human rights monitoring bodies, have more frequently supported amnesties than publicly criticised them.[70] Recent years have also seen cases of international support for amnesty processes. For example, a 2011 statement by the President of the UN Security Council after noting that the Lord's Resistance Army had been responsible for "violations of international humanitarian law and human rights abuses" stated

> The Security Council encourages the remaining LRA members to leave the group's ranks and take advantage of offers of reintegration support. Over the course of the LRA's existence over 12,000 combatants and abductees have left the LRA's ranks and have been reintegrated and reunited with their families through Uganda's Amnesty Commission. The Security Council emphasises its support for continued efforts across the affected countries to disarm, demobilise and reintegrate former LRA fights back into normal life.[71]

This statement did not refer to prosecuting and punishing LRA members responsible for international crimes. In addition, in a 2013 statement to the UN Security Council, Hilde Johnson, Special Representative of the Secretary-General and Head of the United Nations Mission in the Republic of South Sudan described an amnesty granted by the South Sudan government to leaders and members of armed groups as "a very positive development for stability in the country, and in particular for Unity and Upper Nile states."[72] These endorsements of amnesties appear to be motivated by a recognition of the role that amnesty can play in encouraging combatants to surrender and disarm.

In addition, as noted above, states have consistently failed to prohibit amnesty laws in international conventions. Furthermore, in the 2012 Declaration of the High-Level Meeting of the General Assembly on the Rule of Law at the National and International Levels, the UN member states affirmed their commitment to the rule of law and emphasised its importance to peace and agreement, but made no mention of amnesties.[73] This omission is surprising as the UN Secretary General has repeatedly called for a rejection of amnesties in his statements on the rule of law.[74] Furthermore, although some national courts, particularly in South America, have found that amnesties violate their nation's constitutions or international legal obligations,[75] in general, national courts have been more likely to uphold the legality of national amnesty laws.[76]

In sum, state practice suggests that states remain willing to enact amnesty laws and endorse amnesties in other states, even for the most serious crimes, and have consistently rejected proposals to limit their discretion in this area. In addition, amnesties for serious crimes have been upheld by some national courts. On this basis, in keeping with the views expressed by some hybrid courts, paragraph (d) concludes that no settled prohibition on amnesties exists under customary international law.

International Human Rights Law

The duty to prosecute and punish is not explicitly mentioned in universal or regional human rights treaties. Instead, with respect to gross human rights violations, human rights courts and quasi-judicial bodies that monitor compliance with these treaties have read the duty to prosecute into the explicit duty on states to provide a remedy for human rights violations.[77] The UN Human Rights Committee has issued many significant opinions on the status of amnesties under the International Covenant on Civil and Political

Rights, however, paragraph (e) focuses on the case law of human rights courts with binding jurisdiction, namely the Inter-American Court of Human Rights and the European Court of Human Rights.

These courts have taken different approaches on whether there is an obligation to prosecute gross violations of human rights. The Inter-American Court has developed a rejection of broad, unconditional amnesties for serious human rights violations.[78] Its jurisprudence has confirmed that where gross human rights violations have occurred, states must investigate, try, and where appropriate punish those responsible, and provide reparations to victims. The court has not ruled on conditional amnesties or amnesties that are combined with prosecutions. When it considered the reduced sentence regime for crimes against humanity created by the Justice and Peace Law in Colombia, the court rejected requests from the victims' lawyers to find that that it violated the convention.[79] Furthermore, as noted above, a concurring opinion in the *El Mozote v El Salvador* case acknowledged that post-conflict states might need to balance the duty to prosecute against victims' right to peace.

Unlike its Inter-American counterpart, the European Court of Human Rights has no direct experience of dealing with amnesties. Where it has confronted cases of serious human rights violations, the court has declined to proclaim an outright duty to prosecute. Instead, in the 1996 *Aksoy v Turkey* case, the European Court of Human Rights said that with respect to violations of the right to life "the notion of an 'effective remedy' entails a thorough and effective investigation capable of leading to the identification and punishment of those responsible."[80] The phrase "capable of leading to" describes the quality of the investigation, rather than imposing an obligation on the state to prosecute and punish those responsible. In recent decisions, the Court has commented, obiter, that amnesties for war crimes and torture committed by state agents would not be permissible under international law.[81] However, in *Tarbuk v Croatia* the Court held even in such fundamental areas of the protection of human rights as the right to life, the State is justified in enacting, in the context of its criminal policy, any amnesty laws it might consider necessary, with the proviso, however, that a balance is maintained between the legitimate interests of the State and the interests of individual members of the public.[82]

To date, the court has not ruled directly on whether a specific national amnesty is compatible with the European Convention on Human Rights. However, it can be inferred that the court might be tolerant of amnesties for gross human rights violations, such as violations of the right to life, and of amnesties that are enacted to deliver legitimate state interests such as achieving peace and reconciliation, and which seek to fulfil the needs of victims by for example facilitating investigations.[83]

In conclusion, Paragraph (e) emphasises that regional differences exist in the duty to prosecute under international human rights law and that as a result, the legality and legitimacy of amnesties enacted in different parts of the world would be subject to different standards.

Guideline 7. Eligible Offences

The purpose of Guideline 7 is to provide guidance on the offences to be covered in amnesties. To minimise the potential for the amnesty to conflict with any applicable domestic or international law, paragraph (a) recommends that the criteria for determining which offences can be amnestied be clearly specified and limited. Paragraph (b) illustrates some options for limiting the material scope of amnesties including explicitly excluding crimes from the amnesty; limiting the amnesty to an exhaustive list of offences; or granting amnesty for a non-exhaustive category of offences such as political crimes but with guidelines on how this should be interpreted.

Approaches used in amnesty legislation to distinguish political offences from common crimes have included limiting the amnesty to an exhaustive list of specified political offences, such as: treason; counter-insurgency; sedition; forgery; anti-government propaganda; possessing illegal weapons; espionage; membership of banned political or religious organisations; desertion; and defamation.[84] An alternative approach is to grant amnesty for a non-exhaustive list of political offences but with guidelines on how to distinguish political from ordinary offences.[85] To date, the most thorough consideration of political crimes relating to amnesty laws occurred in South Africa.[86] In line with the Guideline 5, on the designing amnesties to complement selective prosecutions, paragraph (b) notes that where crimes are excluded from the amnesty, they remain liable for prosecution and it that may be possible for an individual offender to benefit from an amnesty for eligible offences but to remain liable for prosecution for ineligible offences. This paragraph should be read together with the discussion in Guideline 16 on the creation of amnesty implementation processes to determine whether offences or offenders are eligible for amnesty.

Paragraph (c) highlights crimes that are commonly excluded from amnesties: namely, international crimes and other serious acts of violence against persons,[87] and crimes committed for personal gain or malice.[88] This paragraph notes that excluding international crimes or other serious acts of violence might enhance the legitimacy and legality of the amnesty. However, due to the flexibility in the duty to prosecute and the context-specific nature of a state's obligations outlined above, and a recognition of the positive roles that amnesties can play in conflict or transitional settings (see Guideline 4), the drafters declined to articulate an absolute rule on excluding any categories of offences.

Guideline 8. Eligible Offenders

Guideline 8 addresses the personal scope of amnesties. Paragraph

(a) notes that depending on an amnesty's purposes (see Guideline 4), and applicable requirements of international and domestic law, an amnesty can be designed to target different groups of individuals. In keeping with the approach elsewhere in the Guidelines, the personal coverage of the amnesty should be made explicit and limited. Amnesties can specify categories of persons who are eligible or illegible for amnesty. The identification of categories can be made on a range of bases including affiliation, rank and age.

Affiliation

In identifying potential amnesty beneficiaries by affiliation, distinctions are commonly drawn between state and non-state actors. However, within these broad categories, amnesties can distinguish further by identifying persons based on their membership of particular institutions, political organisations or armed groups. Distinctions by affiliation may depend on the legal status of the persons concerned as state and non-state actors can be treated differently under domestic and international law. Under domestic law, state forces generally have a monopoly on the legitimate use of force, whereas armed opposition groups are usually prohibited. As a result, guerrilla forces may be liable for prosecution for engaging in combat whereas state forces could be portrayed as upholding, rather than breaching the law. Measures such as indemnity laws and emergency laws may also limit the criminal liability of state forces with the result that "state agents may have less need of amnesty than non-state actors."[89] International human rights law has traditionally been viewed as covering only the actions of states *vis-à-vis* their citizens, but not those of private actors, such as non-state armed groups.[90] This distinction is evident in the Convention Against Torture and the Convention for the Protection of All Persons from Enforced Disappearance, which apply only to crimes committed by state agents.[91] In contrast, where offenders commit international crimes, they can be liable for prosecution regardless of affiliation. Paragraph (c) recommends that amnesty design should take into account the existence or absence of liability for different categories of offenders.

Rank or Perceived Level of Responsibility of Offenders

Amnesties may distinguish offenders based on their rank within state institutions or non-state entities. Such distinctions can also be based on offenders' perceived level of responsibility for notorious or egregious crimes. Distinctions based on rank may explicitly exclude high-ranking offenders, whilst granting amnesty to lower-level offenders,[92] or may use a combination of amnesty, trials and other transitional justice mechanisms to address different levels of responsibility among offenders.[93]

Guideline 8(d) refers to the principle of command responsibility as formulated in the Rome Statute[94] and the prosecutorial strategies of international and hybrid courts that emphasise the importance of prosecuting those who are "most responsible,"[95] as potential models for identifying high-ranking individuals to be excluded from amnesties. The drafters declined in Guideline 8(d) to state that amnesties for high-ranking individuals are *prima facie* illegal and illegitimate due to recognition that in some circumstances amnesties these individuals may be required to remove them from public office and prevent them from disrupting the transition. Furthermore, the transitions in South Africa and Northern Ireland provide examples of instances where former leaders of armed groups have played a valuable leadership role in transitions.

In addressing amnesty for lower-level offenders, paragraph (c) refers to international criminal law standards on superior orders.[96] It also invokes standards on excluding criminal liability[97] and mitigating factors, which can apply to offenders of all ranks.[98] These provisions illustrate that there are recognised grounds for relieving or reducing punishments based on the individual circumstances or actions of the offender, even for the most serious offences. Guideline 8(c) recommends that these grounds could in some circumstances justify the use of amnesties for lower-level offenders.

Age

Drawing on the provisions of the Convention of the Rights of the Child (CRC), paragraph (d) states that special attention should be paid in amnesties to the treatment of children responsible for acts that may qualify as national or international crimes. This should consider whether children are below the minimum age of criminal responsibility at the time they committed their offences.[99] Children who have not reached the age of criminal responsibility are not liable for prosecution and hence do not require an amnesty. In many contexts, accessing reintegration programmes may be dependent on participation in an amnesty process. Where children are exempted from these processes, there may be a case for the creation of separate structures to take account of their particular needs.

Children who are above the minimum age of criminal responsibility but below 18 years at the time they committed their offences may be liable for prosecution. The Convention on the Rights of the Child recommends that "whenever appropriate and desirable," states should employ "measures for dealing with such children without resorting to judicial proceedings, providing that human rights and legal safeguards are fully respected."[100] In line with the CRC, paragraph (f) highlights that these children can be included in amnesties but recommends that their particular needs should be addressed in rehabilitation and reintegration programmes.

Guideline 9. Temporal Scope

Start and End Dates

The scope of amnesty laws can be limited by specifying a period of application within which the offences eligible for amnesty were committed, with crimes falling outside this period remaining liable for prosecution. To avoid ambiguity and overly broad interpretations of their scope, in specifying this period of application, the amnesty should clearly state the start date (ie the date after which the crimes must have been committed), and the end date (ie the date by which the crimes must have been committed). Such clear dates are explicit in the amnesties for Chile,[101] Brazil,[102] Nicaragua,[103] and Albania 1997.[104]

Enforced Disappearances

The crime of enforced disappearances has been characterised as a continuous crime in international treaties[105] and the case law of domestic and international courts.[106] This means that the crime begins at the time of the disappearance and continues until the fate or whereabouts of the disappeared person is made known.[107] Drawing on these standards, Guideline 9(b) provides amnesties cannot bar investigations while the fate of the disappeared person remains unresolved.

Guideline 10. Geographic Scope

Where violence and criminality primarily affected one region of a country, it may be appropriate to limit the scope of the amnesty by including only crimes committed within that region.[108] Depending on the levels and patterns of violence across the nation's territory, it may be appropriate for the amnesty to specify that it applies to the whole territory of a state.[109] Where geographic scope is not stated, there is an "implied presumption" that the amnesty covers all eligible crimes irrespective of where they were committed.[110] In a few instances, amnesties have explicitly granted immunity for crimes that were committed outside the territory of the state.[111] As noted in Guideline 18, courts in the states where the crimes were committed or international courts can disregard these amnesties.

5. AMNESTY CONDITIONS

Guideline 11. Prior Conditions on Amnesty Beneficiaries

As discussed in Guideline 1, international crimes and gross human rights violations give rise to multiple legal obligations for states. To enhance an amnesty's legitimacy and legality, Guideline 11 recommends that amnesty beneficiaries be required to participate in mechanisms to comply with a state's obligations to investigate crimes, hold offenders accountable, provide reparations to victims and prevent further violations. Guideline 11 draws on state practice to identify possible prior conditions. In recommending that, where appropriate, prior conditions require individual participation with these mechanisms, it draws on evidence from truth commissions and DDR programmes that the availability of amnesty removes obstacles to offenders participating genuinely in these processes and as a result enhances their work.[112]

Individual Applications

Paragraph (a) notes that individual offenders may be required to submit individual applications. The level of information required in these applications will depend on the objectives of the process, and can include requiring offenders to provide details of the crimes they committed.[113]

Disarmament, Demobilisation and Reintegration (DDR)

Where amnesties aim to reduce violence or end conflict, as discussed in Guideline 4, paragraph (b) notes that they can be conditional on participation in DDR programmes.[114] Examples of amnesties in which offenders were required to disarm and demobilise include Congo in 1999;[115] Aceh in 2005;[116] and Solomon Islands in 2000.[117]

Traditional or Restorative Justice

Guideline 11(c) is derived from the growing recognition within international policymaking and practice of the value of traditional or restorative approaches in addressing criminality or wrongdoing in transitional or post-conflict societies.[118] The mandates, composition, processes and outcomes of restorative mechanisms vary considerably between communities. Academic literature identifies core elements of restorative justice to include:[119] (1) emphasising the harms caused by the offenders' actions to the victims and the wider community; (2) seeking to repair the harms, rather than punishing offenders; (3) recognising that causing harms creates responsibilities for offenders to right their wrongs; (4) seeking to reintegrate offenders and through reintegration, to break cycles of recidivism; and (5) encouraging the participation of all stakeholders including the victims, the offenders, their families, and their wider communities in the identification of harms and the development of remedies. The remedies imposed by restorative processes can include public identification and the imposition of obligations to perform community services, to contribute to financial compensation for victims, or to apologise publicly.

Truth Recovery

In recent years, it has been contended that states have a duty to investigate gross human rights violations, and that, victims and societies affected by such violations have a right to truth.[120] As with the duty to prosecute, the duty to investigate is not articulated in international treaties, but has been developed by universal and regional human rights courts. Where amnesties prevent investigations, they have been found to violate states' obligations to investigate.[121] Paragraphs (d), (e), (f) and (g) highlight that amnesties can be conditioned on offenders engaging with truth-recovery processes to disclose information on their own actions and the actions of others.[122] Such processes can take many forms including: truth commissions; public inquiries; civil proceedings; "truth trials" before criminal courts that do not lead to criminal sanctions; coroners inquests; human rights ombudsmen or human rights commission investigations; traditional or restorative justice mechanisms; and national archive projects. No international court has reviewed the legality of amnesties offered in exchange for testimony, but international conventions and the practice of international criminal tribunals[123] allow for reduced penalties to facilitate truth recovery, even for the most serious crimes. For example, the Convention on Enforced Disappearances allows states parties to establish "mitigating circumstances" for persons "who, having been implicated in the commission of an enforced disappearance, who effectively contribute to bringing the disappeared person forward alive or make it possible to clarify cases of enforced disappearance or to identify the perpetrators of an enforced disappearance."[124]

Reparations

The right to reparations is generally not explicitly outlined in international human rights conventions. Instead, human rights courts have read it into the "right to a remedy" contained in universal and regional human rights treaties.[125] Although international criminal courts do not have the power to order states to pay reparations, the right to reparations is a recognised component of their work.[126] Paragraphs (h) and (i) identify that amnesties can be conditioned on individual offenders contributing to reparations programmes through restitution, financial contributions and community service.[127] Where non-state actors are required to contribute to reparations programmes, this does not to excuse the state from its responsibility to make reparations.

Guideline 12. Conditions of Future Conduct on Amnesty Beneficiaries

Guideline 12 addresses concerns that granting amnesty will create a culture of impunity in which offenders will feel able to reoffend without risk of sanction. Paragraph (a) sets out examples of how amnesties can impose conditions that individual beneficiaries must adhere to in order to retain an amnesty after it is granted. These conditions are designed to ensure the offenders' continued engagement with processes of peacebuilding and reconciliation and to prevent recidivism. The value of such conditions was recognised by the Sierra Leonean Truth and Reconciliation Commission in its final report.[128] For conditions regulating the future conduct of amnesty beneficiaries to be effective, Guideline 12(d) recommends that a formal, independent procedure be established to review or adjudicate compliance, and that where an individual amnesty is revoked, prosecutions should be pursued for the amnestied offences as well as, if applicable, perjury or any subsequent offences.

Adhering to the Conditions on which Amnesty was Granted

Guideline 12(a)(i) suggests that amnesties can be revoked if offenders breach the conditions on which amnesty was granted or if it becomes known that they failed to fulfil them originally. For example, revocations could apply to individuals who were required to disclose their offences fully, it if later becomes known that they withheld or distorted information. As noted in Guideline 12(b), this provision should be read alongside Guideline 11 relating to the prior conditions. Examples of amnesty that explicitly provide for the revocation based on non-compliance include Algeria 1999[129] and Colombia 2005.[130]

Refraining from Violence and Criminality

Guideline 12(a)(ii) provides that amnesty can be revoked, where it is conditional on individual combatants surrendering, ceasing their criminal and/or violent activities, and abiding by national laws, if these individuals return to violence and criminality. The range of crimes that will trigger the loss of the amnesty should be stipulated in the amnesty legislation. Many amnesty laws contain non-recidivism clauses.[131]

Prohibitions on Specified Behaviours

Amnesties can be made conditional on beneficiaries adhering to permanent or temporary restrictions on their behaviour. Such restrictions could prohibit the amnestied person from carrying weapons or joining political organisations. The conditions could be designed to complement processes of vetting[132] by restricting the eligibility of amnestied persons to join the armed forces, work in public sector posts or stand for election. Examples of amnesties that impose conditions on beneficiaries' future behaviour include Algeria in 2006;[133] and Haiti.[134] Restrictions on individual's post-amnesty behaviour should be expressly stipulated in the amnesty text.

Temporary Immunity

Guideline 12(c) suggests an alternative approach whereby temporary immunity defers the decision on prosecutions until the end of an agreed period, when conditions may be more stable and the judiciary may be capable of conducting high-profile prosecutions in a fair and effective manner. When the period of temporary immunity expires, the actions of individual beneficiaries should be evaluated to determine whether they should be liable for prosecution, eligible for permanent amnesty or face an alternative outcome.[135] The legislation providing for temporary immunity should stipulate the duration of the immunity, as well as the criteria for permanent amnesty to be granted or withheld. If during the period of temporary immunity, individuals engage in prohibited behaviours, the temporary immunity should be lifted immediately.[136] Examples of states that have used temporary immunity provisions include South Africa 1990,[137] Burundi 2003[138] and the DRC 2003.[139]

6. AMNESTY ADOPTION, IMPLEMENTATION AND REVIEW

Guideline 13. Adherence to Domestic Law

Guideline 13 recognises that some domestic constitutions provide rules that govern the adoption of amnesty laws.[140] These rules can include whether the executive, or legislature, or both are empowered to grant amnesty; the types of legislative or policy instruments that can be used to grant amnesty; whether it must be adopted by a special voting procedure; which crimes or individuals can benefit from amnesty; and whether it can apply pre or post-conviction. Where an amnesty does not comply with these domestic rules, national courts may declare it unconstitutional or require that it be amended so that it conforms to the appropriate standards.[141]

Guideline 14. Method of Enactment and Public Consultation

Legal Instruments

The instruments by which an amnesty is granted can range from an executive policy, to executive decrees, statutes, and amnesties that are entrenched within constitutions. Guideline 14(a) notes that amnesties that are entrenched within constitutions are harder to amend or annul the amnesty. Guideline 17 addresses the annulment of amnesties.

Public Consultation

Guideline 14(b) draws on the growing recognition of the importance of public consultation in the design and implementation of transitional justice programmes.[142] It draws on experiences to date to suggest commonly used methodologies and it recommends that, to the greatest extent possible, amnesty design should involve public participation, including the involvement of potentially marginalised groups. The extent to which consultation is viable depends on factors such as security levels, infrastructural capacity and whether conditions permit the free circulation of information and opinions. Examples of amnesties that have been adopted as part of deliberative processes include Timor Leste[143] and South Africa.[144] Public participation may enhance the legitimacy of an amnesty, but paragraph (d) notes that public participation is not sufficient by itself to guarantee the legality of an amnesty that otherwise violates domestic or international law.[145]

Referenda

Paragraph (c) draws on state practice where amnesty has been endorsed through a public vote. This could take the form of a referendum on a peace agreement or constitution that contains amnesty provisions,[146] or a referendum that exclusively focuses on the amnesty.[147] Referenda can stimulate public debate on the amnesty and the past crimes that it covers, and where the amnesty is adopted, its legitimacy can be enhanced. However, depending on its scope and the enacting state's legal obligations, as noted in paragraph (d), a referendum in itself would not be sufficient to transform an illegitimate amnesty into a legitimate one.[148]

Self-Amnesties

The term "self-amnesty" denotes amnesties adopted unilaterally by regimes that have often seized power illegally, are responsible for international crimes or gross violations of human rights, and which use the amnesty protect the public officials and their supporters from all forms of investigation and accountability for human rights violations. Self-amnesties have received the greatest scrutiny from the organs of the Inter-American system, which have found them to violate the American Convention on Human Rights.[149] In line with the characterisation of illegitimate amnesties in Guideline 4(b), Guideline 14(d) recommends that self-amnesties should be regarded as *prima facie* illegitimate and illegal.

Guideline 15. Legal Effects

The primary effect of amnesties is of course to prevent criminal prosecutions. However, Guideline 15(a) draws on state practice to illustrate that amnesties may have a range of other legal effects. As noted in the discussion of Guideline 13, these effects may correspond to domestic law governing the use of amnesties and as discussed below, they may blur the distinctions between amnesties and other forms of leniency, such as pardons.

These legal effects can apply uniformly to all amnesty beneficiaries, or can be used to distinguish between different categories of beneficiaries. For example, offences that are more serious may receive sentence reductions, whereas less serious offences may obtain full amnesty. Guideline 15(c) recommends that it may be beneficial to vary the legal consequences of an amnesty among offenders to reflect the gravity of their actions.

Amnesties can require the police or prosecution services to refrain from launching criminal investigations of persons or crimes that are eligible for amnesty. This can benefit offenders who have not been identified. Barring the opening of criminal investigations does not necessarily preclude offenders being investigated by other truth recovery processes. Examples of amnesties that prevent criminal investigations include Algeria 1999;[150] Bahrain 2001;[151] Federation of Bosnia and Herzegovina 1999;[152] Mexico 1994;[153] Tajikistan 1997;[154] and Burma 2008.[155] Recent experiences in Chile suggest that where amnesties do not explicitly preclude criminal investigations, domestic judiciaries may reinterpret the amnesty to require that investigations be conducted to determine an individual's eligibility before the amnesty is applied.[156]

Where amnesties are enacted when criminal investigations and trials are ongoing, their legal effects may include closing proceedings that are open. If the amnesty is conditional on individual offenders performing specified acts, the trial may be postponed or suspended until they have completed these acts, and it will only be definitely closed once all conditions have been fulfilled. Examples of amnesties that have closed ongoing criminal proceedings include the Federation of Bosnia-Herzegovina 1999;[157] El Salvador 1987;[158] Macedonia 2002;[159] Namibia 1989;[160] Peru 1995;[161] and Bangladesh 1997.[162]

Although amnesties are conceptually distinct from leniency measures that apply post-conviction, in practice many amnesties apply to both persons who have been convicted and persons who have not been subject to any legal proceedings. The effects of post-conviction amnesties may include immediate and unconditional release from punishment; release on probation or suspended sentence; sentence reduction; or a combination of these measures tiered to take into account the gravity of individual offenders' actions. Examples of post-conviction amnesties that applied uniformly to all convicted prisoners include El Salvador;[163] Peru;[164] Democratic Republic of Congo;[165] and Côte d'Ivoire.[166] Where amnesties are granted to persons who have previously been convicted, they have in some instances been used to expunge their criminal record.[167]

Amnesty can impede victims' ability to access civil remedies in two ways. Firstly, the amnesty may explicitly provide immunity from civil liability. Examples of such amnesties include Argentina 1983;[168] El Salvador 1993;[169] and Sudan 1997.[170] Secondly, an amnesty may indirectly prevent victims obtaining redress in legal systems where the availability of such redress is dependent upon the existence of a prior criminal conviction. In contrast, the following examples expressly exempt immunity from civil actions from the scope of the amnesty: Argentina 1986;[171] Philippines 1994;[172] and Democratic Republic of Congo 2005.[173] Guideline 15(b) recommends that where an amnesty bars civil liability, administrative reparations should be developed to provide remedies to victims. As noted in Guideline 11, individual offenders could be required to contribute to these programmes.

Guideline 16. Administering the Amnesty

Implementation Process

The implementation of limited, conditional amnesties requires the creation of administrative processes to assess the eligibility of individuals. Guideline 16(a) reviews the forms that such implementation processes could take and recommends minimum standards that should be in place for the implementation to be effective, transparent and legitimate. These standards draw on recognised best practice that is generally prescribed for truth commissions[174] and the experiences of amnesty implementing processes in diverse states. For example, critiques of the Amnesty Committee of the South African Truth and Reconciliation Commission indicate that where an amnesty is conditional on offenders fully disclosing the truth about their actions, the amnesty implementing body should be granted sufficient powers to enable it to corroborate and challenge the accounts provided by amnesty applicants.[175] This could, for example, require an amnesty commission to have powers to search premises, take statements, seize documents, subpoena witness and require cooperation from other government departments.

Victim and Community Participation

Guideline 16(b) builds on the commitment to public participation outlined in Guideline 14(b) and the principles of restorative justice described above, to recommend that where possible, victims and civil society organisations be allowed to participate in hearings on individual applications for amnesty. Drawing on the experience of the Amnesty Committee of the South African Truth and Reconciliation Commission, this Guideline recommends measures to facilitate participation.[176]

Right of Appeal

To respect the procedural rights of individual amnesty applicants,

Guideline 16(c) recommends that they are granted the right to appeal decisions of the amnesty implementing body to independent courts.

Guideline 17. Annulling Amnesties

Guideline 17 is motivated primarily by the annulment of amnesties in Argentina, Peru and Uruguay over the past decade. These amnesties all offered automatic and unconditional immunity for gross human rights violations. Their annulment was achieved through one or several of the following: judgments by the Inter-American Court;[177] domestic judicial decisions declaring the law unconstitutional;[178] and national legislation to annul the amnesty.[179] The annulments had retroactive effect that enabled cases that had previously been closed by the amnesties to be reopened. To allow for the possibility of future annulment, Guideline 17(a) notes that an amnesty could make provision for future domestic judicial review.

Guideline 17(b) draws on the experience of Chile where the impunity created by the 1978 amnesty law has been narrowed through a range of judicial reinterpretations. Early in the transition, limitations and exceptions contained in this amnesty were not consistently applied by the courts. Recent jurisprudence has entailed inter alia applying these exceptions and reinterpreting the amnesty in light of international legal developments.[180] Although the Chilean amnesty has not been annulled, these reinterpretations have allowed the reopening of cases that were previously closed by the amnesty. At the time of writing, more cases have been reopened in Chile, than in the countries where the amnesties have been annulled.[181] This Guideline therefore notes that reopening cases may not require the annulment of an amnesty.

Guideline 18. International Courts and National Amnesties

Jurisdiction to Rule on Foreign Amnesties

Where individuals who have benefited from an amnesty have become the subject of criminal proceedings before an international or foreign court, a limited case law has developed where these individuals have sought to invoke amnesty to argue that the court has no jurisdiction, and that to proceed with the prosecution would be an abuse of process. These cases indicate that with respect to unconditional amnesties for international crimes, foreign courts do not consider themselves bound to recognise amnesties enacted elsewhere.[182] The ICTY,[183] the Special Court for Sierra Leone[184] and the Extraordinary Chambers of the Courts of Cambodia[185] have adopted similar positions. Guideline 18(a) concurs with this approach by stating that amnesties cannot bar international, hybrid or foreign courts from exercising jurisdiction.

International Criminal Tribunals, Hybrid Courts and National Amnesties

Paragraph (b) emphasises the duties on states to cooperate with international criminal courts. Paragraph (c) then draws on the practice of countries such as Sierra Leone, Timor Leste and Cambodia to note that although international criminal courts can convict individuals who have benefited from an amnesty, this does not result in the amnesty ceasing to have effect for other offenders (see Guideline 3).

Regional Human Rights Courts

Paragraph (d) notes that human rights courts can evaluate the extent to which an amnesty complies with a state's obligations under applicable treaties. As explored in the discussion of Guideline 6(e), the Inter-American Court of Human Rights has been most active in considering amnesties. Where it has found that an amnesty violates the American Convention on Human Rights, it has recommended a range of remedies including annulling amnesties (see Guideline 17). In the case of Peru, this resulted in the amnesty ceasing to have effect;[186] however, similar rulings on the amnesties in Chile and Brazil have not been given effect by national authorities.

7. CONCLUSION

The Belfast Guidelines on Amnesty and Accountability seek to move discussion of the legality of amnesties from a predominant focus on the duty to prosecute to consider the relationship of amnesties to the full range of legal obligations incumbent on conflicted and transitional states. In addition, they aim to enhance human rights protections by recommending ways in which amnesties can be designed to contribute to peace, truth, accountability and reconciliation. To enhance their accessibility the guidelines will be translated into Arabic, French, Mandarin, Russian and Spanish. It is hoped that the guidelines will be widely disseminated and will be of value to individuals and organisations that are grappling with decisions on how to deal with legacies of violent pasts.

1   Rodrigo Uprimny Yepes (Director, Center for the Study of Law, Justice and Society (Dejusticia); and Associate Professor of Law at Universidad Nacional de Colombia); María Paula Saffon (Ph. Candidate, Columbia University, Department of Political Science; and Associate Researcher, Dejusticia); and Nelson Camilo Sánchez (Research Coordinator, Dejusticia; and Associate Professor of Law at Universidad Nacional de Colombia) were invited to represent the views of Latin Americans within the Expert group and contributed to the discussions but did not feel able to endorse the final version.

2   The Explanatory Guidance by Louise Mallinder is published with these Guidelines. The Commentary also by Mallinder will be published as a book in 2014.

3   "Gross violations of human rights" is used here to denote acts that constitute serious crimes under national or international law and, if committed by a government, would violate the state's human rights obligations. This includes the most serious actions that are prohibited in universal and regional human rights treaties, such as torture and other cruel, inhuman or degrading treatment; extra-judicial, summary or arbitrary executions; slavery; enforced disappearances. It also includes rape and other forms of sexual violence, which depending on circumstances, can be forms of war crimes or torture.

4   See eg Robert Parker, *Fighting the Siren's Song: The Problem of Amnesty in Historical and Contemporary Perspective*, 42 Acta Juridica Hungaria 69 *(2001)*; KATHLEEN DEAN MOORE, PARDONS: JUSTICE, MERCY AND THE PUBLIC INTEREST (1997).

5   Protocol Additional to the Geneva Conventions of 12 August 1949, and relating to the Protection of Victims of Non-International Armed Conflicts (Protocol II), Jun. 8, 1977, 1125 UNTS 609.

6   COMMENTARY ON THE ADDITIONAL PROTOCOLS OF 8 JUNE 1977 TO THE GENEVA CONVENTIONS OF 12 AUGUST 1949 (Yves Sandoz et al. ed., 1987) ¶ 4618.

7   UN Econ. & Soc. Council, Sub-Comm. on Prevention of Discrimination & Prot. of Minorities, *Resolution 1983/34. The administration of justice and the human rights of detainees.* UN Doc E/CN.4/Sub.2/RES/1983/34 (Sep. 6, 1983).

8   UN Econ. & Soc. Council, Sub-Comm. on Prevention of Discrimination & Prot. of Minorities, *Study on Amnesty Laws and their Role in the Safeguard and Protection of Human Rights*, UN Doc E/CN.4/Sub.2/1985/16 (Jun. 21, 1985).

9   *Id.*

10 See eg UNSC Res. 861, UN Doc. S/RES/861 (Aug. 27, 1993) (supporting the Governors' Island Agreement in Haiti); Douglass Cassel, *Lessons from the Americas: Guidelines for International Response to Amnesties for Atrocities,* 59 Law & Contemp.Probs. 197 (1996) (on UN support for amnesties in El Salvador and Guatemala); Michael P. Scharf, *From the eXile Files: An Essay on Trading Justice for Peace,* 63 Wash.& Lee L.Rev. 339 (2006) (on UN brokering the asylum for Charles Taylor).

11 See discussions of Guidelines 1 and 6 for analysis of these obligations.

12 OHCHR, *Rule of Law Tools for Post-Conflict States: Amnesties,* UN Doc HR/PUB/09/1 (2009).

13 See Guideline 6.

14 *Id.*

15 WILLIAM SCHABAS, UNIMAGINABLE ATROCITIES: JUSTICE, POLITICS, AND RIGHTS AT THE WAR CRIMES TRIBUNALS, 197-8 (2012); MARK FREEMAN, NECESSARY EVILS: AMNESTIES AND THE SEARCH FOR JUSTICE, 27-8 (2010).

16 Freeman, *supra* note 15, at 25.

17 TRICIA D. OLSEN et al., TRANSITIONAL JUSTICE IN BALANCE: COMPARING PROCESSES, WEIGHING EFFICACY, 154 (2010).

18 *Id.* at 154.

19 *Id.* at 154.

20 Nathan Ricci, *Eroding the Barrier between Peace and Justice: Effects of Transitional Justice Mechanisms on Post-Conflict Stability* (Centre for Mediation, Peace and Resolution of Conflict, 2012).

21 Where attributes of particular amnesties are discussed here, this should not be interpreted as a reflection that the amnesty cited is an example of best practice per se, but rather that certain aspects of the amnesty's design illustrate possible positive approaches.

22 Vienna Declaration and Programme of Action, U.N. Doc. A/CONF.157/24 (1993).

23 International Law Commission, *Fragmentation of International Law: Difficulties arising from the Diversification and Expansion of International Law,* ¶24, UN Doc A/CN.4/L.682 (Apr. 13, 2006).

24 *Id.* at ¶36.

25 International Law Commission, *Conclusions of the work of the Study Group on the Fragmentation of International Law: Difficulties arising from the Diversification and Expansion of International Law* (2006) ¶4, http://untreaty.un.org/ilc/texts/instruments/english/draft%20articles/1_9_2006.pdf.

26 SCHABAS, *supra* note 15, at 186-7.

27 Massacres of El Mozote and nearby places v El Salvador, Inter-Am Ct HR (Oct. 25, 2012), Concurring opinion of Judge Diego García-Sayán, ¶¶37-38. See also *Nydia Erika Bautista de Arellana v Colombia*, Comm. No. 563/1993, UNHRC, UN Doc CCPR/C/55/D/563/1993 (1995), ¶8.6 and Prosecutor v Allieu Kondewa, Case No. SCSL-2004-14-AR72(6), Decision on lack of jurisdiction / abuse of process: amnesty provided by the Lomé Accord ¶40 (May 25, 2004) (on the right to remedy not equating to a right for victims to force state to prosecute). See also mitigating factors in sentencing at the international criminal tribunals discussed in Guideline 8.

28 See eg UN Secretary General, *Secretary-General's "An Age of Accountability" address to the Review Conference on the International Criminal Court,* May 31, 2010, http://www.un.org/sg/statements/?nid=4585.

29 STEVEN R. RATNER et al., ACCOUNTABILITY FOR HUMAN RIGHTS ATROCITIES IN INTERNATIONAL LAW: BEYOND THE NUREMBERG LEGACY, 15-16 (3rd ed. 2009).

30 Ruth W. Grant & Robert O. Keohane, *Accountability and Abuses of Power in World Politics,* 99 Amer. Pol. Sci. Rev. 29 (2005); Mark Philp, *Delimiting Democratic Accountability,* 57 Pol. Stud. 28 (2009); DECLAN ROCHE, ACCOUNTABILITY IN RESTORATIVE JUSTICE (2004); Louise Mallinder & Kieran McEvoy, *Rethinking Amnesties: Atrocity, Accountability and Impunity in Post-Conflict Societies,* 6 Contemp. Soc. Sci. 107 (2011)

31 Stanley Cohen, *Unspeakable Memories and Commensurable Law, in* LEGAL INSTITUTIONS AND COLLECTIVE MEMORIES, 27 (Susanne Karstedt ed., 2009)

32 UNSC, *Report of the Secretary-General on the Rule of Law and Transitional Justice in Conflict and Post-Conflict Societies,* UN Doc S/2004/616 (2004)

33 *Id.* at ¶ 46.

34 Morten Bergsmo, *The Theme of Selection and Prioritization Criteria and Why it is Relevant, in* CRITERIA FOR PRIORITIZING AND SELECTING CORE INTERNATIONAL CRIMES CASES 15 (Morten Bergsmo ed., 2009); ROBERT CRYER, PROSECUTING INTERNATIONAL CRIMES: SELECTIVITY AND THE INTERNATIONAL CRIMINAL LAW REGIME (2005)

35 Loi relative à la mise hors-la-loi de la clique du Kampuchea democratique, art. 1 (1994) (Cambodia).

36 UN Department of Peacekeeping Operations, Disarmament, Demobilization and Reintegration of Ex-Combatants in a Peacekeeping Environment: Principles and Guidelines (UN 1999) Annex 2B, 109.

37 See eg Kieran McEvoy & Louise Mallinder, *Amnesties in Transition: Punishment, Restoration and the Governance of Mercy,* 39 Journal of Law and Society 410 (2012).

38 Secretary-General, *supra* note 32, at ¶ 32.

39 UNHCR, *Legal Safety Issues in the Context of Voluntary Repatriation,* ¶12, UN Doc EC/54/SC/CRP.12 (Jun. 7, 2004).

40 Prosecutor v Ieng Sary, Case File No. 002/19-09-2007/ECCC/TC, Decision on Ieng Sary's Rule 89 Preliminary Objections (*Ne Bis in Idem* and Amnesty and Pardon), ¶ 52 (Nov. 3, 2011).

41 *Id.* at ¶ 52.

42 *Id.* at ¶ 53.

43 See eg SCHABAS, *supra* note 15, at 175; Jessica Gavron, *Amnesties in the Light of Developments in International Law and the Establishment of the International Criminal Court,* 51 Int'L & Comp.L.Q. 91 (2002)

44 UN. Econ. & Soc. Council, *Report of the Intersessional Open-ended Working Group to Elaborate a Draft Legally Binding Instrument for the Protection of all Persons from Enforced Disappearance,* ¶¶ 73-80, UN Doc E/CN.4/2004/59 (Feb. 23, 2004).

45 During an early stage of the negotiations on Article 6(5), the USSR proposed that this article could not be construed to permit amnesty for war crimes or crimes against humanity. However, this interpretation was rejected by the

other states who expressed views that amnesty was an exercise of sovereign prerogative and desirable to promote reconciliation. See OFFICIAL RECORDS OF THE DIPLOMATIC CONFERENCE ON THE REAFFIRMATION AND DEVELOPMENT OF INTERNATIONAL HUMANITARIAN LAW APPLICABLE IN ARMED CONFLICTS, GENEVA (1974-1977).

46 CHRISTINE BELL, ON THE LAW OF PEACE: PEACE AGREEMENTS AND THE LEX PACIFICATORIA (2008)

47 There are of course areas of overlap between the regimes, for example, torture is both an international crime and a gross human rights violation.

48 Convention on the Prevention and Punishment of the Crime of Genocide, Dec. 9, 1948, 78 UNTS 1021.

49 Geneva Conventions, Aug. 12, 1949: Common art. Common art. 49 (Geneva I); 50 (Geneva II); 129 (Geneva III); and 146 (Geneva IV); Protocol Additional to the Geneva Conventions and relating to the Protection of Victims of International Armed Conflicts (Protocol I), Jun. 8, 1977, art. 84.

50 Convention against Torture and Other Cruel, Inhuman or Degrading Treatment, Dec. 10, 1984, 1465 UNTS 85 ("Convention Against Torture").

51 International Convention for the Protection of All Persons from Enforced Disappearance, Dec. 20, 2006, G.A. res. 61/177, U.N. Doc. A/RES/61/177 ("Convention on Enforced Disappearances").

52 Article 7(2) of the Convention Against Torture and Article 11(2) of the Convention on Enforced Disappearances.

53 Statute of the International Court of Justice, art. 38, June 26, 1945, 33 U.N.T.S. 993.

54 Prosecutor v Furundžija, Judgement, Case No. IT-95-17/1-T, ¶ 155 (Dec. 10, 1998); Prosecutor v Radovan Karadžić, Case No. IT-95-5/18-PT, Decision on the Accused's Second Motion for Inspection and Disclosure: Immunity Issue, ¶¶ 17 and 25 (Dec. 17, 2008) and Decision on Karadžić's Appeal of Trial Chamber's Decision on the Alleged Holbrooke Agreement, ¶ 52 (Oct. 12, 2009).

55 Cited in Prosecutor v Morris Kallon, Brima Bazzy Kamara, Case No. SCSL-2004-15-PT-060-I, Decision on challenge Lomé Accord Amnesty, ¶ 71 (13 Mar. 2004). See also *Prosecutor v Allieu Kondewa*, Decision on Lack of

Jurisdiction/Abuse of Process: Amnesty Provided by the Lomé Accord, filed under Case No. SCSL-2004-14-AR72(E) (25 May 2004). *But cf* Prosecutor v Augustine Gbao, Decision on Preliminary Motion on the Invalidity of the Agreement between the United Nations and the Government of Sierra Leone on the Establishment of the Special Court, SCSL-04-15-PT-141 (25 May 2004).

56 Decision on Ieng Sary's Rule 89 Preliminary Objections, *supra* note 40, at ¶ 53.

57 ICJ Statute, Article 38(1)(d).

58 See eg Commission on Human Rights, *Updated Set of principles for the protection and promotion of human rights through action to combat impunity*, UN Doc E/CN.4/2005/102/Add.1 (Feb. 8, 2005); UN Commission on Human Rights, *Basic Principles and Guidelines on the Right to a Remedy and Reparation for Victims of Gross Violations of International Human Rights Law and Serious Violations of International Humanitarian Law*, UN Doc A/RES/60/147(Mar. 21, 2006); African Commission on Human and Peoples' Rights, *Guidelines and Measures for the Prohibition and Prevention of Torture, Cruel, Inhuman or Degrading Treatment or Punishment in Africa* (Oct. 23, 2002).

59 ANTHONY AUST, HANDBOOK OF INTERNATIONAL LAW (2nd ed. 2010)

60 Alan Boyle, *Soft Law in International Law Making, in* INTERNATIONAL LAW 122 (Malcolm D. Evans ed., 3rd ed.2010)

61 Common Article 3 to the Geneva Conventions 1949.

62 CUSTOMARY INTERNATIONAL HUMANITARIAN LAW (Jean-Marie Henckaerts & Louise Doswald-Beck eds., 2005)

63 *Id.* at Rule 159.

64 *Id.* at Rule 158.

65 *Id.* at Rule 159.

66 *Id.* Volume Two of this study looks at "Practice."

67 Data is gathered in relation to international crimes only when (1) the crimes were explicitly mentioned in the text of the amnesty; (2) when case law indicated that the amnesty included or excluded crimes under international

law; and/or (3) when there is substantial evidence in reports by UN, regional human rights institutions or by respected human rights organisations, such as Amnesty International or Human Rights Watch, that crimes under international law were perpetrated.

68 Louise Mallinder, *Amnesties' Challenge to the Global Accountability Norm? Interpreting Regional and International Trends in Amnesty Enactment, in* AMNESTY IN THE AGE OF HUMAN RIGHTS ACCOUNTABILITY: COMPARATIVE AND INTERNATIONAL PERSPECTIVES Leigh A. Payne & Francesca Lessa eds., 2012)

69 As the Amnesty Law Database only gathers data relating to amnesty laws that were formally enacted, this data does not include contexts were amnesties were proposed but ultimately rejected following international condemnation.

70 LOUISE MALLINDER, AMNESTIES, HUMAN RIGHTS AND POLITICAL TRANSITIONS, 335-7 (2009).

71 UNSC, *Statement by President of the Security Council*, UN Doc S/PRST/2011/2 (Nov. 14, 2011).

72 UNSC, *Report of the Secretary General on South Sudan*, UN Doc S/PV.6993 (Jul. 8, 2013).

73 UNGA, Resolution 67/1 Declaration of the High-level Meeting of the General Assembly on the Rule of Law at the National and International Levels, UN Doc A/RES/67/1 (Nov. 30, 2012).

74 See eg UN Press Release, *Reject Endorsement of Amnesties for Serious Crimes, Gross Human Rights Violations, Secretary General urges Security Council in Meeting on Rule of Law*, UN Doc SG/SM/14069 (Jan. 19, 2012).

75 See Guideline 17.

76 See eg *Azanian Peoples Organization (AZAPO) v the President of the Republic of South Africa* (CCT 17/96) (8) BCLR 1015 (CC) (S. Afr.); Corte Suprema de Justicia, Guevara Portillo (Aug. 16, 1995) (El Sal.); Thomas Kwoyelo alias Latoni v Uganda, Constitutional Court of Uganda, Petition No. 036/11, (Sep. 21 2011) (Uganda); Supremo Tribunal Federal, ADPF 153 – arguição de descumprimento de preceito fundamental (2010) (Brazil); Tribunal Supremo, Sentencia Absolutoria, Sentencia No: 101/2012 (Feb. 27, 2012) (Spain).

77 See eg International Covenant on Civil and Political Rights, art. 2(3), Dec. 16, 1966, 999 UNTS 171.

78 See eg Barrios Altos Case (Chumbipuma Aguirre et al v Peru), Inter-Am. Ct. H. R. (ser. C) No. 74 (2001) ¶ 41; Myrna Mack Chang v Guatemala, Inter-Am. Ct. H. R. (ser. C) No. 101 (2003) ¶ 153; Almonacid-Arellano et al. v. Chile, Inter-Am. Ct. H. R. (ser. C) No 154 (2006) ¶ 114; *Gomes Lund v Brazil*, Inter-Am. Ct. H. R. (2010); Gelman v. Uruguay, Inter-Am. Ct. H. R. (ser. C), No. 221 (2011) ¶ 241.

79 See eg Rochela Massacre v Colombia, Inter-Am. Ct. H. R. (ser. C) No. 175 (2008).

80 Aksoy v. Turkey, judgment of 18 December 1996, *Reports of Judgments and Decisions* 1996-VI ¶ 98. This formulation has been used in numerous subsequent judgments by the ECtHR.

81 Abdülsamet Yaman v Turkey, App No. 32446/96, Eur. Ct. H. R. (2004) ¶ 55. See also *Tuna v Turkey*, App. No. 22339/03, Eur. Ct. H. R. (2010) ¶ 71; *Ely Ould Dah v France*, App. No 13113/03 Eur. Ct. H. R. (2009); Marguš v Croatia, App. No. 4455/10, Eur. Ct. H. R. (2012), ¶ 74.

82 Tarbuk v Croatia, App. No. 31360/10 Eur. Ct. H. R. (2012) ¶ 50.

83 Legal Status of Amnesty, Third party intervention in the case of Marguš v. Croatia, Application no. 4455/10 (May 29, 2013) (on file with the author).

84 See eg Indo-Sri Lanka Accord, ¶ 2.11, 1987.

85 Ley de Reconciliación Nacional, art. 2, 1996 (Guat.).

86 Promotion of National Unity and Reconciliation Act, s 20.3, 1995, (S. Afr.).

87 See eg Loi d'Amnistie, art. 3, 2009 (Dem. Rep. Congo); Ordonnance no 2007-457 (Côte d'Ivoire); Proclamation No. 75, s 1, 2010 (Phil.); Ley de Amnistía Politica General, art. 4, 2000 (Venez.); Loi d'amnistie générale, 2008 (Cent. Afr. Rep.); Act No. 6 Truth, Justice and Reconciliation Act, s 34(3), 2008 (Kenya); Decreto de amnistía a quienes participaron en el golpe de Estado de Honduras. No 2-2010, art. 1 (Hond.).

88 See eg Law No. 4616 on the conditional release and the suspension of trials and sentences for offences committed up until 23 April 1999 (Turk.); Resolution of the Supreme Assembly of Tajikistan "On Amnesty for Participants in the Political and Military Confrontation in the Republic of Tajikistan," 1997 (Taj.); Ley de Amnistía General para la Consolidación de la Paz, Decree No 486, 1993 (El Sal.); Decree "On Amnesty to Persons who

Staged Socially-Dangerous Actions in Connection with the Armed Conflict in the Chechen Republic," 1997 (Russ.).

89 FREEMAN, *supra* note 15, at fn 268.

90 LIESBETH ZEGVELD, ACCOUNTABILITY OF ARMED OPPOSITION GROUPS IN INTERNATIONAL LAW, 38 (2002)

91 Convention on Enforced Disappearances, art. 2 and Convention Against Torture art. 1(1).

92 Eg Presidential Decree 519, 1974 (Greece); Loi Relative à la mise hors-la-loi de la clique du Kampuchéa Démocratique, 1994 (Cambodia).

93 Eg in Timor-Leste the most serious offenders were tried before the Serious Crimes Panel of the District Court of Dili, other offenders testified before the truth commission, and the lowest level offenders engaged in Community Reconciliation Process through which they could be awarded amnesty. In Rwanda, those accused of genocide were placed into categories according to the type of crime committed and their level of participation. These categories regulated whether individuals would be held accountable by national courts or non-judicial gacaca courts, and the penalties that could be imposed. See Organic Law no. 16/2004 and Organic Law no. 10/2007 (Rwanda).

94 Rome Statute of the International Criminal Court, art. 28, 2187 U.N.T.S. 90 (Jul. 17,1998).

95 ICC Office of the Prosecutor, *Prosecutorial Strategy 2009-12*, ¶ 19 (2010); See eg ICTY, *Rules of Procedure and Evidence*, r 28(A) (2006); Statute of the Special Court of Sierra Leone, art. 1 (2000); The Law on the Establishment of the Extraordinary Chambers in the Courts of Cambodia for the Prosecution of Crimes Committed During the Period of Democratic Kampuchea, art. 1 (2001).

96 Rome Statute, at art. 33; Henckaerts & Doswold-Beck, *supra* note 62, at Rule 155.

97 Rome Statute, at art. 31.

98 ICC, Rules of Procedure and Evidence, Rule 145 (2002).

99 Convention on the Rights of the Child, art. 40(3), 1577 UNTS 3 (Nov. 20, 1989).

100 *Id.*, at art. 40(3).

101 Decreto Ley 2,191, 1978 (Chile).

102 Lei N 6.683 Concede anistia e dá outras providências, 1979 (Braz.).

103 Ley de amnistía general y reconciliación nacional, 1990 (Nicar.)

104 Law on Amnesty for civilians and military personnel who were involved in the riots after the collapse of fraudulent pyramid schemes, Law No. 8198, 1997 (Alb.).

105 Convention on Enforced Disappearance, art. 24(6).

106 See eg Velasquez Rodriguez Case, ¶ 181, Inter-Am.Ct.H.R. (Ser. C) No. 4 (1988).

107 Working Group on Enforced or Involuntary Disappearances, *General Comment on Enforced Disappearance as a Continuous Crime*, ¶ 1, UN Doc A/HRC/16/48 (2010).

108 See eg Ley de Amnistía, 1994 (Mexico); Law "On Amnesty for People who Committed Crimes during the Counter-Terrorist Operation in the Caucasus," 1999 (Russ.); Presidential Decree No 1082, 1977 (Phil.); Loi d'Amnistie, 2009 (Dem. Rep. Congo); Proclamation of Amnesty for Niger Delta Militants, 2009 (Nig.).

109 See eg Law on General Amnesty, No 80/96, 1996 (Croat.).

110 FREEMAN, *supra* note 15, at 162.

111 See Loi portant amnistie, art. 1, 2003 (Côte d'Ivoire); Loi No 66-396 portant amnistie d'infractions contre la sûreté de l'Etat ou commises en relation avec les événements d'Algérie, 1966, (Fr.); Promotion of National Unity and Reconciliation Act, art. 20(2), 1995 (S. Afr.).

112 See eg Secretary-General, *supra* note 32, at ¶ 32 (on amnesties and DDR); *Azanian Peoples Organisation (AZAPO) and others v the President of the Republic of South Africa and others* 1996 (4) SA 671 (CC), ¶ 17 (S. Afr.); TRC Report, Vol 1, ch 5, ¶ 66 (S. Afr).

113 See eg Promotion of National Unity and Reconciliation Act 1995, s 18(1) (S. Afr.).

114 The Secretary-General, *Disarmament, Demobilization and Reintegration: Report of the Secretary-General*, ¶ 24, UN Doc A/60/705 (Mar. 2, 2006).

115 Loi No. 21-99, art. 3, 1999 (Dem. Rep. Congo).

116 Memorandum of Understanding between the Government of the Republic of Indonesia and the Free Aceh Movement, 15 Aug 2005, implemented in Presidential Decree N° 22/2005 on general amnesty and abolition of Free Aceh Movement, 2005 (Indo.).

117 Amnesty Act, No. 3, art. 3(3) (2000) (Solomon Is.).

118 Secretary-General, *supra* note 32, at ¶ 12.

119 See eg Howard Zehr, *Doing Justice, Healing Trauma: The Role of Restorative Justice in Peacebuilding*, 1 S. Asian J. Peacebuilding (2008); Stephan Parmentier et al., *Dealing with the Legacy of Mass Violence: Changing Lenses to Restorative Justice, in* SUPRANATIONAL CRIMINOLOGY: TOWARDS A CRIMINOLOGY OF INTERNATIONAL CRIMES 335 (Smeulers Alette & Haveman Roelof eds., 2008); Jennifer J. Llewellyn, *Restorative Justice in Transitions and Beyond: The Justice Potential of Truth Telling Mechanisms for Post-Peace Accord Societies, in* TELLING THE TRUTHS: TRUTH TELLING AND PEACE BUILDING IN POST-CONFLICT SOCIETIES 83 (Tristan Anne Borer ed., 2006)

120 See eg OHCHR, *Study on the Right to Truth*, ¶ 8, UN Doc E/CN.4/2006/91 (Feb. 8, 2006).

121 See eg Rodríguez v. Uruguay, Communication No. 322/1988, U.N. Doc. CCPR/C/51/D/322/1988 (1994), ¶ 12.4; UN Human Rights Committee, Basilio Laureano Atachahua v. Peru, Communication No. 540/1993, U.N. Doc. CCPR/C/56/D/540/1993 (1996), ¶ 8.3; Consuelo et al. v. Argentina, Case 10.147, 10.181, 10.240, 10.262, 10.309, 10.311 Report No. 28/92, Inter-Am.C.H.R., OEA/Ser.L/V/II.83 Doc. 14 at 41 (1993) ¶ 42; Parada Cea v. El Salvador, Case 10.480, Inter-Am. C.H.R., Report No. 1/99, OEA/Ser.L/V/II.106, doc. 6 rev. (1999) ¶ 146; Samuel Alfonso Catalán Lincoleo v. Chile, Case 11.771, Report No. 61/01, OEA/Ser.L/V/II.111 Doc. 20 rev. at 818 (2000), ¶¶ 72-3; Carmen Aguiar de Lapaco v. Argentina, Case 12.059, Report No. 21/00, (2000) ¶ 17; Almonacid-Arellano et al. v. Chile, Inter-Amer. Ct. H.R., (ser. C) No. 154, ¶ 114 (2006); Gomes Lund v Brazil, Inter-Am. Ct. H.R., ¶ 138 (2010).

122 See Promotion of National Unity and Reconciliation Act 1995 (S. Afr.); Regulation No. 2001/10 on the Establishment of a Commission for Reception, Truth and Reconciliation in East Timor (2001) (Timor-Leste) s 1.

123 Eg ICTY, Prosecutor v Erdemovic, Case No. IT-96-22-Tbis, ¶ 21 (1998).

124 Convention on Enforced Disappearances, art. 7(2).

125 See eg Velásquez Rodríguez v Honduras - Compensatory Damages, Inter-Am. Ct. H. R. (ser. C) No. 7 (1989) ¶ 26; Castillo Páez v Peru – Reparations, Inter-Am. Ct. H. R. (ser. C) No. 43 (1998) Barrios Altos Case (Chumbipuma Aguirre et al v Peru) – Reparations, Inter-Am. Ct. H. R. (ser. C) No. 87 (2001) ¶ 42; Myrna Mack Chang v Guatemala, Inter-Am. Ct. H. R. (ser. C) No. 101 (2003).

126 See eg Rules of Procedure and Evidence of the ad hoc tribunals, Rule 106; and Rome Statute, art. 75. See also *UNGA, Basic Principles and Guidelines on the Right to a Remedy and Reparation for Victims of Gross Violations of International Human Rights Law and Serious Violations of International Humanitarian Law*, Res. 60/147 (2005).

127 See eg Corte Constitucional, Sentencia C-370/06 (May 18, 2006) (Colom.); Commission for Reception, Truth and Reconciliation, *Chega! The CAVR Report*, ch 9, ¶ 112, 2005 (Timor Leste).

128 Truth and Reconciliation Commission of Sierra Leone, Final Report, Volume Three B, Chapter Six: The TRC and the Special Court for Sierra Leone, ¶ 26, 2004.

129 Loi no 99-08 relative au rétablissement de la Concorde civile, art. 8, 1999 (Alg.).

130 Ley 975, art. 25, 2005 (Colom.).

131 See eg Amnesty (Amendment) Act, 2002 (Uganda); Loi d'amnistie générale n° 84/91, art. 2, 1991 (Leb.).

132 See eg OHCHR, *Rule of Law Tools for Post-Conflict States: Vetting – An Operational Framework*, UN Doc UN Doc HR/PUB/06/5 (2006).

133 Ordonnance no 06-01 portant mise en oeuvre de la Charte pour la paix et la reconciliation nationale (2006) art. 26 (Alg.).

134 1993 Governors Island Agreement, UN Doc S/26063 (1993). Implemented in Loi relative à l'amnestie, 1994 (Haiti).

135 Ronald C. Slye, *A Limited Amnesty? Insights from Cambodia*, in AMNESTY IN THE AGE OF HUMAN RIGHTS ACCOUNTABILITY: COMPARATIVE AND INTERNATIONAL PERSPECTIVES 291 (Francesca Lessa & Leigh Payne eds., 2012).

136 *Id.*

137 Indemnity Act 1990, s 1(1) (S. Afr.).

138 Loi No 1/022 portant immunite provisoire de poursuites judiciaries en faveur des leaders politiques rentrant d'exil, 2003 (Burundi).

139 Decret-Loi portant amnistie pour faits de guerre, infractions politiques et d'opinion, 2003 (Dem. Rep. Congo). This immunity was made permanent in 2005. See Loi portant amnistie des personnes responsables de faits de guerre, des infractions politiques et de délits d'opinion, 2005 (Dem. Rep. Congo).

140 See eg Ethiopian Constitution, art. 28(1) (1994); Constitution of Ecuador, art. 80 (2008); Constitution of Venezuela, art. 29 (1999).

141 See eg Constitutional Court Decision on the TRC Law, Decision Number 006/PUU-IV/2006 (Dec. 6, 2006) (Indon.).

142 See eg OHCHR, *Rule of Law Tools for Post-Conflict States: National Consultations on Transitional Justice*, UN Doc HR/PUB/09/2 (2009); Working Group on Enforced or Involuntary Disappearances, *General comment on article 18 of the Declaration*, ¶ 8, UN Doc E/CN.4/2006/56 (2005).

143 See eg Amy Senier, *Traditional Justice as Transitional Justice: A Comparative Case Study of Rwanda and East Timor* (2008) XXIII Praxis 67, 76.

144 ALEX BORAINE, A COUNTRY UNMASKED: INSIDE SOUTH AFRICA'S TRUTH AND RECONCILIATION COMMISSION (2000); JEREMY SARKIN, CARROTS AND STICKS: THE TRC AND THE SOUTH AFRICAN AMNESTY PROCESS (2004).

145 See OHCHR, *supra* note 12, at 41.

146 See eg Constitution of Ghana, First Schedule, s. 34, 1992.

147 See eg Jo-Marie Burt, Gabriela Fried Amilivia & Francesca Lessa, *Civil Society and the Resurgent Struggle Against Impunity in Uruguay (1986–2012)*, 7 Int'L J. Transitional just. (2013).

148 Gelman v. Uruguay, Inter-Am. Ct. H. R. (ser. C), No. 221, ¶¶ 238-9 (2011).

149 See eg Barrios Altos Case, Inter-Am. Ct. H.R. (ser. C) No. 75, ¶ 43 (2001). See also *Loayza Tamayo v. Peru*, Reparations and Costs, Inter-Am. Ct. H. R. (ser.

C), No. 42, ¶¶ 167-8 (1998). Almonacid-Arellano et al v Chile, Inter-Am. Ct. H. R. (ser. C) no. 154, ¶ 120 (2006)

150 Law No. 99-08, art. 36, 1999 (Alg.).

151 Legislative Decree No. 10, 2001 (Bahrain).

152 Law on Amnesty, No 48/99, 1999 (Federation of Bosn. & Herz.).

153 Ley de Amnistía, Ley 1/21/94 (Mexico).

154 Resolution "On Amnesty for Participants in the Political and Military Confrontation in the Republic of Tajikistan", 1997 (Taj.).

155 Constitution of the Republic of the Union of Myanmar, 2008, Chp 14, s 445.

156 See eg Marny A. Requa, *A Human Rights Triumph? Dictatorship-Era Crimes and the Chilean Supreme Court,* 12 Hum. Rts L. Rev 79 (2012); CATH COLLINS, POST-TRANSITIONAL JUSTICE: HUMAN RIGHTS TRIALS IN CHILE AND EL SALVADOR (2010).

157 Law on Amnesty, Official Gazette No 48/99 (3 Dec 1999) [Federation Law].

158 Ley de Amnistía para el Logro de la Reconciliación Nacional, 1987 (El Sal.).

159 Law on Amnesty, 2002 (FYR Macedonia).

160 Amnesty Proclamation, 1989 (Phil.).

161 Ley N° 26479 Conceden amnistía general a personal militar, political y civil para diversos casos, 1995 (Peru).

162 Chittagong Hill Tracts Peace Treaty, 1997 (Bangl.).

163 Ley de Amnistía para el Logro de la Reconciliación Nacional, 1987 (El. Sal.).

164 Ley N° 26479 Conceden amnistía general a personal militar, political y civil para diversos casos, 1995 (Peru).

165 Law No 05-023, art. 1, 2005 (Dem. Rep. Congo).

166 Ordonnance no 2007-457, Article 4, 2007 (Côte d'Ivoire).

167 See eg Promotion of National Unity and Reconciliation Act, s 20(10), 1995 (S. Afr.).

168 Ley de Pacificación Nacional, No. 22.924, art. 6 (1983) (Arg).

169 Ley de Amnistía General para la Consolidación de la Paz, No 486, art. 4(e), 1993 (El. Sal.).

170 Khartoum Peace Agreement, Annex 2 "General Amnesty Proclamation Order", art. 2 (Sudan).

171 Ley de Punto Final, No. 23.495, art. 6, 1986 (Arg.).

172 Amnesty Proclamation No 347, 1994 (Phil).

173 Law No 05-023, art. 4, 2005 (Dem. Rep. Congo).

174 See eg OHCHR, *Rule of Law Tools for Post-Conflict States: Truth Commissions* UN Doc HR/PUB/06/1 (2006).

175 See eg TRUTH AND RECONCILIATION IN SOUTH AFRICA: DID THE TRC DELIVER?(Audrey R. Chapman & Hugo Van der Merwe eds., 2007).

176 See eg ANTJE DU BOIS-PEDAIN, TRANSITIONAL AMNESTY IN SOUTH AFRICA, 223-4 (2007).

177 See eg Barrios Altos Case (Chumbipuma Aguirre et al v Peru), Inter-Am. Ct. H. R., (ser. C) No. 74 (2001); Gelman v. Uruguay, Inter-Am. Ct. H. R. (ser. C), No. 221 (2011).

178 Resolución del Juez Federal Gabriel R. Cavallo declarando la inconstitucionalidad y la nulidad insanable de los arts. 1 de la Ley de Punto Final y 1, 3 y 4 de la Ley de Obediencia Debida ("Simón Julio") No. 17.768, 2001 (Arg.);

179 Law No. 18.831, 2011 (Uru.); Law No. 25.779, 2003 (Arg.).

180 See eg Pedro Enrique Poblete Córdova, Corte Suprema, Rol. 469-98 (1998) English translation is in 2 *Yearbook of International Humanitarian Law* 485 (1999) (Chile).

181 See Human Rights Observatory, *Latest Human Rights Case Statistics for Chile*, http://www.icso.cl/observatorio-derechos-humanos/cifras-causas-case-statistics/

182 See eg Orden de prisión provisional incondicional de Leopoldo Fortunato Galtieri por delitos de asesinato, desaparición forzosa y genocidio, Audiencia

Nacional, 1997 (Spain); Anto de la Sala de lo Penal de la Audiencia Nacional confirmado la jurisdicción de España para conocer de los crimenes de genocidio y terrorismo comtedidos durante la dictadura argentina, Audiencia Nacional, 1998 (Spain). See also *Ely Ould Dah*, Tribunal de Grande Instance de Montpellier, 2001 (Fr.); *Ely Ould Dah*, Court of Cassation, 2002 (Fr.); Expediente de extradición 5/2000, Juez Sexto de distrito de Procesos Penales en el Distrito Federal, Resolution 5/2000, 2001 (Mex.).

183 Prosecutor v. Anto Furundžija, ¶ 155; Prosecutor v Radovan Karadžić, Decision on the Accused's Second Motion for Inspection and Disclosure: Immunity Issue, Case No. IT-95-5/18-PT ¶ 17 (2008).

184 Decision on challenge to jurisdiction, *supra* note 55, at ¶ 67.

185 Decision on Ieng Sary's Rule 89 Preliminary Objections, *supra* note 40, at ¶ 53.

186 Resolución de la Corte Interamericana de Derechos Humanos de 22 de Septiembre de 2005, Caso Barrios Altos, Cumplimiento de Sentencia.